Tower Hamlets College
Learning Centre

115997

Nasser

D1354929

Nasser

Anne Alexander

HAUS PUBLISHING • LONDON

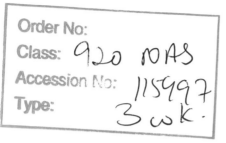

Order No:

Class: 920 NAS

Accession No: 115997

Type: 3 wk.

First published in Great Britain by
Haus Publishing Limited
26 Cadogan Court
Draycott Avenue
London SW3 3BX

A CIP catalogue record for this book
is available from the British Library

ISBN 1-904341-83-7 (paperback)

Designed and typeset in Garamond and Futura by Andrea El-Akshar, Köln

Printed and bound by Graphicom in Vicenza, Italy

Front cover: Time Magazine cover, 26 September 1955, courtesy of
        Time Life pictures/Getty Images
Back cover: Egypt Historical Archive

Contents

A childhood at the end of empire

Later, he would have the scar airbrushed out of his official photographs. But as a seventeen-year old student leader he wore the mark left on his forehead by a police officer's bullet as a badge of honour. Along with thousands of other Egyptian schoolboys, Gamal Abd-al-Nasser's first experience of political organisation came with a maelstrom of demonstrations in 1935 and 1936. Two students were killed, and Gamal was lucky to escape with only a graze.

The protests left a permanent mark on Egyptian political life. More than a rite-of-passage, 1936 represented a turning point for a generation. It was the moment when Egypt's political centre of gravity moved out of the corridors of parliament into the street. After 1936, the liberal politicians and imperial civil servants who hoped to trammel Egypt's nationalist movement would find themselves swimming against a slowly rising tide.

Many years later Nasser wrote that 1936 was the year he lost faith in Egypt's leaders. *In those days I led demonstrations from al-Nahda school, shouting at the top of my voice for complete independence, with many others following behind. But our cries died into faint echoes, blown away by the winds. We moved no mountains and cracked no rocks. Then I decided that 'positive action' meant uniting all the leaders of Egypt behind a single slogan. So our chanting, rebellious crowd went round to their homes, one by one, demanding in the name of Egypt's youth, that they come together. They did unite on one issue, but their decision destroyed my faith – they agreed to conclude the Treaty of 1936.*[1]

Like an old scar under the skin, 1936 changed the face of Egypt.

Cotton ginning

The Empire and Egypt

The Foreign Office mandarins who drew up the Anglo-Egyptian Treaty of 1936 seem to have regarded the document as an exercise in tidying up the historical record. Under the agreement, Egypt's independence was confirmed and the country entered the League of Nations. The all-powerful High Commissioner became simply the British Ambassador, British control of the Egyptian army was relaxed and the officer corps opened to ordinary citizens – a decision which was to play an important part in Nasser's own life.

Yet for many Egyptians, the 1936 Treaty was a betrayal of their hopes for real independence. After half a century of occupation, Nasser and his classmates wanted an end to British power in Egypt, not the semi-colonial status promised by the Treaty. The roots of their adolescent rage lay in the tangled history of European imperial ambitions in the Middle East.

Long before Britain occupied Egypt in 1882, European capital and European imperial power had begun to shape the Egyptian economy. Muhammad Ali, an Albanian mercenary who founded Egypt's last dynasty in the early 19th century, was the first in the Middle East to challenge European economic penetration. Although he represented the Ottoman Sultan in Istanbul, Muhammad Ali sought to carve out an independent role for himself and his heirs. He conquered the Hejaz and Syria, sent expeditionary forces to Sudan, and began to develop industries to compete with the European goods flooding local markets.

In 1839 Muhammad Ali sent his army against his masters in Istanbul, prompting a European intervention to save the Ottoman Empire from collapse. Defeated in battle, Ali was forced to dismantle the tariff barriers, which had protected his fledgling local industries from European competition. The years after his death saw increasing European investment in what became one of the 'emerging markets' of the day. On the stock exchanges of London and Paris, investors rushed to buy shares in fashionable projects, such as the Suez Canal.

After British forces occupied Alexandria in 1882, cotton secured Egypt a place in Britain's imperial economy, with the Nile plantations providing the raw material for Lancashire spinning mills.

By the end of the 19th century, many areas of Egypt's economy had been skewed towards the cotton economy. Those sectors of agriculture and transport concerned with the production and transport of raw cotton developed quickly, while other areas stagnated.

For French engineers and investors the Canal was a symbol of progress and enlightenment. Egyptians saw it rather differently. Egypt's ruling family – heirs of Muhammad Ali now relegated to the status of mere governors, or Khedives – press-ganged tens of thousands of construction workers. Forced labour still played a central role in Egypt's semi-feudal agricultural system and thousands toiled to ensure that European investors collected their dividends on time. Yet despite mortgaging Egypt to the hilt to pay for the canal, the Khedival family saw little return on its investment.

In 1854, Said Pasha, the Ottoman Vice-Regent of Egypt, granted the French engineer Ferdinand de Lesseps the right to dig and operate the Suez Canal.

This alliance between Muhammad Ali's heir and French capital mobilised twenty thousand Egyptian peasants and millions of francs to construct the waterway.

Burdened by huge debts – generated by extravagant purchases of European machinery and by the ruinous interest rates charged by European bankers – Ismail Pasha sold Egypt's stake in the Canal Company to British Prime Minister Benjamin Disraeli in 1875.

Colonel Urabi's revolt

From the point of view of European speculators, the outlook was far less bleak. In 1878 European administrators took over the running of Egypt's economy to prevent the bankrupt country defaulting on her debts. The Egyptian budget was placed in the hands of an Anglo-French commission of bankers, which increased taxes to pay creditors in London and Paris. Even the *Times* correspondent in Alexandria felt uneasy about the debt collection system. He wrote in 1879 that the produce collected on behalf of the banks 'consists wholly of taxes paid by the peasants in kind, and when one thinks of the poverty-stricken, overdriven, underpaid *fellahin* [peasants] in their miserable hovels, working late and early to fill the pockets of the creditors, the punctual payment of the coupon ceases to be wholly a subject of gratification.'[2]

In the Nile Valley desperate peasants took to banditry. Demonstrations under the slogan 'Egypt for the Egyptians' rocked the major cities. Colonel Ahmad Urabi, a nationalist army officer who criticized Khedive Tawfiq's dependence on European advisers, became the focus of discontent. Demonstrations and petitions forced Tawfiq to invite Urabi into his cabinet as Minister of War. Urabi and his supporters purged the army and government of Europeans and the Khedive's supporters. In May 1882, fearing for their financial interests, Britain and France demanded his dismissal, only to face a popular revolt. Protestors organised an assembly which set up a common-law government and deposed the Khedive, appealing over his head to the Ottoman Sultan in Istanbul.

European troops in Alexandria fired into a crowd on 11 June 1882, leading to several days of rioting which left more than 250 Egyptians and 50 Europeans dead. The London press deplored this outbreak of 'anarchy' which left Alexandria 'in the power of a mob'. [3] British Prime Minister Gladstone responded by sending gunboats to defeat Urabi. The troops would remain in Egypt for more than 70 years.

Egypt under Cromer

The British occupation of Egypt was not graced with an official title until 1915. Until this date Egypt was neither a colony, nor a Protectorate nor a Dominion of the British crown. As P. J. Vatikiotis describes, 'Britain in Egypt was simply, though significantly, a 'presence' astride the Suez Canal and the route to India.'[4] Although Muhammad Ali's heirs still ruled in name, real power lay with the British High Commissioner, Evelyn Baring, Lord Cromer.

Despite this official ambiguity, British occupation changed Egypt. British military control accelerated the integration of Egypt into the world economy, but at a price. Under British occupation Egypt was practically a monoculture: 'a gigantic cotton plantation'[5], in the words of one contemporary writer. Instead of boosting local industry, Egyptian cotton travelled thousands of miles to the mills of Lancashire, before returning to Egypt as cheap cotton clothes. In the imperial supply chain, Egypt's place was fixed as a producer of raw materials and a consumer of finished goods.

Notwithstanding the wealth now flowing through the Egyptian economy, British officials continued the tradition of government austerity, spending little on education and social welfare. In keeping with Egypt's ambiguous status, however,

Cromer's power was exercised through a veiled Protectorate. Occasionally the screen would slip, as it did when the Khedive Abbas II was deposed by the British in 1914. The years before World War One also saw the foundation of Egypt's first political parties and the growth of a modern press. Beyond the intrigues of the court and the colonial administration a nationalist movement was emerging. This triangle of opposing interests – the court, the British High Commission, and the nationalist opposition – would dominate Egyptian politics for more than three decades.

The population of Egypt was still dominated by *fellahin*.

A state of ferment and agitation

British rule did not simply change the economy; it also altered Egyptian society as new social classes began to develop in response to the demands of the imperial economy. A small working class, mainly concentrated in sectors such as transport and public utilities, sprang up in the late 19th century and early 20th century. Despite their small numbers, organised workers played an important role in the nationalist protests of 1919.

More important to the development of an Egyptian nationalist movement was the emergence of a modern middle class. In actual numbers this class represented a small fraction of a population still dominated by peasants, but it played a pivotal role in shaping Egypt's independence movement. The colonial authorities encouraged the development of a European-style education system in order to supply clerks and officials to run the expanding government bureaucracy. This gave the sons, and sometimes even the daughters, of ordinary Egyptians, far greater opportunities for social mobility. It also produced fertile ground for the spread of nationalist ideas. Egyptian clerks working side-by-side with European administrators resented their subordinate status and their lower salaries.

As Egypt's social hierarchies became more fluid under the pressure of economic change, the grip of the country's old ruling class

– the Turco-Circassian Ottoman elite – began to weaken. Under Ottoman rule the ruling family and major landowners, in addition to the top ranks of the army, came from this narrow group. By the late 19th century the grip of the Turco-Circassian elite had been significantly weakened. The decline of the Ottoman Empire itself was a major factor in this change. However, the actions of the European powers, particularly France and Britain, also undermined its rule. European advisers dominated the Ottoman cabinet, and pressure from Britain and France forced government and policy changes on the reluctant Khedives. The loosening of the bonds which kept the old political system together coincided with a ferment of new experiences and ideas. Influences from European culture were most visible in the new government education system, which provided an alternative to the traditional learning of the Koran school and the great mosque university of Al-Azhar in Cairo.

Nasser gave his own view of the contradictory pressures on Egyptian society in *The Philosophy of the Revolution*, the short pamphlet he wrote in 1953, not long after the Free Officers took power. *I sometimes consider the state of an average Egyptian family – one of the thousands of families which live in the capital of the country. The father, for example, is a turbaned fellah – a thorough-bred country fellow. The mother is a lady of Turkish descent. The sons and daughters attend schools respectively following the English and French educational systems. All this is in an atmosphere where the 13th-century spirit and 20th-century manifestations intermingle and interact ... We live in a society not yet crystallized. It is still in a state of ferment and agitation.*[6]

The small village of Beni Murr in the Nile Valley was a long way from the royal court in Cairo, and even further from the British Foreign and Colonial Office in London, yet the social changes brought about by British occupation shaped Nasser's family history. The expansion of education and the growing need for government clerks gave his father, Abd-al-Nassser Hussein, the son of a well-off peasant family, the opportunity to pursue a career in the civil service. In 1914 he moved from his family home in Beni Murr to take up a job as sub-postmaster in a working class district of Alexandria. There he married Fahima, the daughter of a coal merchant. His wife's family were also recent migrants from the Sa'id, southern Egypt, but Abd-al-Nasser's father-in-law had prospered in the city, building up a substantial business. For Abd-al-Nasser the chance to break out of the closed world of the south must have been irresistible. Alexandria, a cosmopolitan Mediterranean city of half a million people, was a world away from village life in Beni Murr.

Abd-al-Nasser was not the only one of his generation to leave the family's farm for the broader horizons of city life. His brother, Khalil, who would later provide a home for Nasser in Cairo, also became a government clerk. Abd-al-Nasser and Fahima settled in a small apartment at 18 Anawati Street in the quiet working-class district of Bacus, behind Ramleh station on the Alexandrian seafront. Their first child, Gamal, was born on 15 January 1918.

Family portrait taken towards the end of Gamal's time at primary school:
He is standing between his father and uncle. (Other children:
his brothers Al-Laithy, Izz-al-Arab, and Shawqi)

1919: the year of revolution

Except for his uncle, Khalil, who was said to have been briefly imprisoned for nationalist activities, none of Nasser's immediate family seem to have been personally affected by the revolution of 1919. But Egyptian political life was profoundly changed by the emergence of a mass nationalist movement, which set the scene for Nasser's turbulent school days and his first political activities.

The outbreak of war in 1914 at first dashed hopes of change. In 1915 Britain formally made Egypt part of the British Empire. Egypt's transformation into a Protectorate at first seemed to have put back hopes of a gradual relaxation of British control. Yet, as the war ended, Egyptian nationalists were encouraged by the speeches of US President Woodrow Wilson, who promised national self-determination for the colonial peoples of the world.

The hero of Egypt's 1919 revolution was born in 1858, in a village in Gharbiya province. Sa'ad Zaghlul initially studied at the Islamic university, Al-Azhar, but later qualified as a lawyer in Paris.

He was appointed Minister of Education in 1906, and then Minister of Justice in 1910. It was after the war that he emerged as Egypt's best-known nationalist leader. His imprisonment and exile at the hands of the British triggered the 1919 uprising.

Zaghlul was also the inspiration behind Egypt's first mass nationalist party, the Wafd, which took its name from his Egyptian delegation – *al-wafd al-misry* in Arabic – to Versailles.

Sa'ad Zaghlul emerged as the spokesman for a reawakened nationalist movement in Egypt. A lawyer by training, he had served as a minister in the pre-war cabinets of Khedive Abbas, trying to extend Egyptian autonomy by gradual reforms. A generation had passed since the crushing of Urabi's rebellion, and middle-class nationalists were beginning to demand more Egyptian control of the country's political life.

At the Versailles peace conference national delegations clamoured for recognition of

Statue of Sa'ad Zaghlul in Alexandria, Egypt's best known nationalist leader

their claims to independence. But behind the façade of Wilsonian rhetoric lay the stark realities of imperial power. Britain and France were weakened by the war but determined to maintain their presence in the Middle East. Newly-discovered oil deposits in Mesopotamia increased the importance of the Suez Canal, Egypt's primary international asset, so when Sa'ad Zaghlul gathered a group of like-minded moderate nationalists to send a delegation to the peace conference, the British High Commissioner refused them permission to represent Egypt. Foreign Office officials in London had their own ideas about who should go to Versailles – their choice for the job was Rushdi Pasha, the prime minister and a solidly pro-British figure. Sa'ad Zaghlul's response was to take the question to the Egyptian people. His Egyptian delegation, *al-wafd al-misry* in Arabic, toured the country. Thousands packed into meetings and rallies to acclaim Zaghlul's *Wafd* as the true representatives of Egypt. Petitions poured into Cairo calling on the British High Commissioner Wingate to allow Zaghlul and his colleagues to travel to France.

The response from the High Commission was to arrest and exile Zaghlul and two companions. Egypt exploded into revolution as strikes and demonstrations shook the major cities. Peasants cut the railways and burnt out rural police stations. According to Bimbasha MacPherson, the British intelligence chief of the Cairo police, students led the first anti-British demonstrations. Trams were stopped and damaged and the depot at Shubra attacked. The Sheikh of Al-Azhar, the Islamic university, gave a sermon calling on the people to throw off the tyrant's yoke. Transport workers joined the protests, and soon school pupils, tram workers, printers and road sweepers were all on strike. After several weeks of rising violence the High Commissioner, realizing that only an all-out assault by the British Army could quell the rebellion, called Zaghlul back from exile.

The Wafd's dilemma

Riding high on a triumphant wave of popular protest, Sa'ad Zaghlul eventually did make it to Versailles. Yet the conference itself was a disappointment, as deals were struck behind the scenes between the imperial powers. It was this process which transformed the British protectorate into a mandate from the newly-founded League of Nations, a purely cosmetic change in the eyes of most Egyptians.

Instead of loosening the grip of the Khedival family on Egypt, Britain strengthened it, creating a monarchy and crowning Fu'ad, a nephew of Khedive Abbas, King of Egypt in 1922. The new monarch's powers to interfere in constitutional life were extended, as the King had the right to dismiss ministers, dissolve parliament and appoint the prime minister. The pill was sugared with a formal declaration of independence in 1922, which nationalists complained meant little, as Britain reserved the right to maintain troops in Egypt and to take whatever action she chose to defend the Canal and British interests in time of war or civil unrest.

Egypt's first experiment in constitutional democracy during the 1920s and 1930s was not a productive one. Political life was dominated by a trio of competing factions: the Wafd, the palace and the British High Commission. The King, hankering after a larger role in politics, was only too happy to oblige the High Commissioner by dissolving unruly nationalist parliaments. As for the Wafd, despite its immense base of popular legitimacy it was also prepared, once in power, to keep the nationalist movement within the bounds set by the British authorities and the King.

The Wafd won 90 percent of the seats in the elections of 1924, although the indirect electoral system favoured establishment candidates. Millions of Egyptians expected the Wafd to be able to bring about far-reaching changes in their lives, but the party's leaders were desperate to avoid social upheaval. So Sa'ad Zaghlul's government crushed the growing trade union movement and stamped out further nationalist agitation. Yet without the mass following which had revolted for its sake in March 1919, the Wafd could not hope to defeat the King and the British. Time and time again, the Wafdist leaders were forced to back mass protests, raising hopes they refused to meet.

On the move

Nasser spent much of his childhood on the move. When he was three, the family moved back to the south, to Assyut. Two years later his father was posted to Khatatba, a small town north-east of Cairo, where Nasser had his first taste of school life. He did not stay long in Khatatba, as his father sent him to Cairo to live with his uncle Khalil, an employee of the Ministry of Religious Endowments. Nasser's three years there were spent in the bustling heart of old Cairo; he used to explore the old bazaars in the shadow of the Al-Azhar mosque and university complex with a friend.

He missed his mother. however, and with the help of his uncle, regularly wrote to her in Khatatba. In 1926, her replies suddenly stopped, although he was reassured to be told that she was merely away from home on a visit to her parents. It was only when he went home several months later that he found out that she had died. He later described the experience as *a cruel blow that was imprinted indelibly on my mind.*[7] His relationship with his father became more distant, particularly after Abd-al-Nasser remarried in 1928. In a family home crowded with younger children – he was the eldest of eleven – he withdrew into a world of his own.

After a brief stay in Alexandria with his grandparents following his father's second marriage, Nasser was sent to boarding school in Helwan, near Cairo. However, he came back in 1929 to re-join the family after his father was transferred to Alexandria once again. It was in Alexandria that he had his first experience of politics. Swept up in a demonstration by older schoolmates belonging to the Young Egypt movement of Ahmad Hussein, he ended up in a police cell overnight, until his father came to rescue him.

In 1933 the family moved again, this time to Cairo, as Abd-al-Nasser took up running the post-office in Khoronfish, in the area of Bab al-Sharqiyyah. For the next four years Nasser attended the Al-Nahdah secondary school. He wrote for the school newspaper, contributing an article on Voltaire, and tried his hand at acting. At the school's performance of Shakespeare's Julius Caesar, Nasser's performance of the dying Roman leader was so realistic, that his father jumped up from the audience and rushed to his aid, before being reassured that his son was unharmed.

Avid reader: Gamal as a schoolboy

Cultural currents

A serious, thoughtful adolescent could find plenty to engage with in 1930s Cairo. Despite continuing political repression, Egypt was going through something of a cultural renaissance. A new generation of writers explored the contradictions created by the modernisation of Egyptian society, re-working the Arabic language with new tools: modern literature, drama, and journalism.

The confident nationalism of the urban middle classes found its ideological expression in rationalist, secular constitutionalism. Writers such as Taha Hussein explored the heritage of Pharaonic Egypt in an attempt to construct a national identity. They associated Islam with the backwardness and superstition, which they believed was holding back national development. However, for most of the population the writers and politicians who held these views were speaking a language which was not only alien, but was also directly associated with colonial oppression.

At school Nasser read avidly. His choice of English authors shows an interest in the lives of great men of history; among the books he read at secondary school were John Buchan's *Gordon in Khartoum*, Winston Churchill's autobiography and the lives of Alexander the Great, German Chancellor Otto von Bismarck and the Italian nationalist Garibaldi.

One of the Egyptian authors who caught Nasser's imagination as a schoolboy was the novelist and playwright Tawfiq al-Hakim. A prolific writer, Al-Hakim turned recently-imported European literary forms such as the novel and the short story into expressions of a new Egyptian culture. This process of literary transformation mirrored Egypt's political awakening.

Often described as the founder of modern Arabic drama, Tawfiq al-Hakim was born to a middle-class family in Alexandria in 1898.

His novel *Return of the Spirit* was acknowledged by Nasser to be his inspiration for the revolution of 1952. According to the novelist Naguib Mahfouz 'the leader that Al-Hakim had envisioned and dreamt of was perceived to be Nasser, and Nasser himself understood it so. Thus he held Al-Hakim in esteem and always treated him graciously.'

Yet Al-Hakim himself always maintained a certain distance from Nasser, turning down an invitation to meet him.

Nasser devoured Al-Hakim's first novel, *Return of the Spirit*, which was published in 1933 to wide acclaim. He identified with Al-Hakim's hero, Muhsin, a sensitive but lonely young man, caught up the excitement of the revolution of 1919. Al-Hakim's portrayal of adolescent love may also have touched a chord, and his understanding of a teenager's need for space to think, dream and grow: 'the freedom and solitude which can only be felt by the person who has a room of his own.'[8] Nasser was also fascinated by the political conclusions Al-Hakim drew from the revolution of 1919. In *Return of the Spirit*, the hopes of the Egyptian people can only find expression in a charismatic leader, identified as Sa'd Zaghlul, leader of the Wafd. One of the characters, a French archaeologist, explains to his sceptical English colleague that the Egyptian people are still destined to achieve great things. 'Do not despise these people, wretched though they are today. Strength is hidden in them. They lack only one thing ... they lack that man in whom all their feelings and desires will be represented, and who will be for them a symbol of their objective. When that happens, do not be surprised at this people - cohesive, united, oppressed and ready for sacrifice - if it produces another miracle besides the pyramids!'[9]

Al-Hakim's second novel, *Diary of a Country Prosecutor*[10] - a dark satire on the criminal justice system - is set in a small village in the Delta. Through the weary eyes of a cynical bureaucrat, the author explores the cruel absurdities of rural life. Yet although Al-Hakim draws an unflattering picture of the long-suffering Egyptian peasants, his sharpest criticisms are reserved for those in authority over them. In Al-Hakim's portrayal, traditional authority figures and the representatives of the modern state and its European legal code conspire together to oppress the fellahin. The arrival of modern technology – the telegraph, the telephone and the railway – merely reinforces the age-old structure of power.

In the *Diary*, Al-Hakim exposes the moral rot at the heart of the state. Corrupt judges and brutal police officers are all engaged in the same great game – swindling the common people. As the district police chief explains, not even elections are left to chance. "Well, that's my method with elections," he continued. "Complete freedom. I let people vote as they like – right up to the end of the elections. Then I simply take the ballot box and throw it in the river and replace it with the box which we prepare ourselves."' [11]

Al-Hakim's central character, the world-weary prosecutor who acts as narrator in the novel, soon learns to suppress his moral qualms and keep his head down. Nasser did not mention reading the *Diary*, but he would have certainly recognised the cynical political establishment Al-Hakim described. Throughout 1935 and 1936 Nasser and his school friends were in all-out rebellion against the same corrupt system. He wrote to a school friend, Hasan al-Nashar, in September 1935, *where are the men ready to give their lives for the independence of the country? ... They say the Egyptian is a coward, that he is afraid of the slightest sound. He needs a leader to lead him in the struggle for his country. By this means this same Egyptian would become a thunder-clap which would make the walls of tyranny tremble.* [12]

Back to the streets

After 1930, Egyptian politics moved back into the streets. The inconclusive struggle between the King, the British and the Wafd dominated parliamentary life. But, unlike in 1919 when the Wafd spearheaded a united national movement, the struggles of the 1930s ended in stalemate. During 1935 and 1936 huge demonstrations called for the restoration of the 1923 constitution, which had been overturned by conservative politicians to give the King even greater powers. The protests were characterized by street fighting between the Muslim Brothers, the pro-Royalist 'Green Shirts' of the Young Egypt movement and the Wafdist 'Blue Shirts'.

The Muslim Brotherhood, which was founded by Hassan al-Banna in 1928, appealed to a sense that modernity carried with it an attack on Islam. Al-Banna argued that foreign domination had to end, and that a truly Islamic society would offer social justice to the poor and downtrodden. The Brotherhood drew its support from the urban poor, but its cadre was the urban lower middle class – students, graduates, teachers, low-ranking officials in government ministries and petty traders, all of whom felt that the promise of modernisation had failed them.

Young Egypt was founded by Ahmad Hussein. The movement called for an end to foreign control of Egypt and agitated for the foundation of an Egyptian empire. European Fascism appeared to be the greatest influence on Young Egypt's political style, however. Its paramilitary parades and celebration of militarism won supporters among the school students, including Nasser himself for a brief period.

The Wafd's return to power in 1936 was also greeted by a wave of industrial unrest, inspired partly by the general strikes in Belgium and France. A huge strike wave began with a stoppage and occupation of the Kafr al-Zayyat oil company which spread to Alexandria, culminating in a tramwaymen's strike. By mid-July, the workers' mobilisation had moved to Cairo with a sudden strike and sit-in closing Hawamidiyya sugar refinery.

Nasser threw himself into organising. During his last year at Al-Nahda he spent only 45 days actually in school. He flirted with most of the political organisations of the day, including both the Brotherhood and Young Egypt, but does not seem to have been impressed by any of them. His greatest disappointment, however, was with the older generation of nationalists, who seemed prepared to sell Egypt's future by bargaining with the British. The treaty gave Egypt more control over her diplomatic affairs and paved the way for her entry into the League of Nations. But the price for these formal steps towards independence was the conclusion of an Anglo-Egyptian military alliance, which gave Britain the right to maintain ten thousand troops in the Canal Zone.

An anti-climax

Despite Nasser's disappointment, the signing of the Anglo-Egyptian Treaty and the accession of a new King, the young prince Farouq, finally dampened the student rebellion. Some held high hopes that the new King would support reforms. 'The new monarch at first seemed everything his father was not – patriotic, vigorous, intelligent and democratically-inclined – and so won immediate and widespread popularity.'[13] Other student leaders, like Nasser himself, turned back to their studies. In Nasser's case, it took a demonstration by his classmates before the headmaster would let him back in the door.

Finishing school left him with another dilemma. The months of student campaigning had left him with a police record, and seemed at first to have blocked the only road he really wanted to take after school: into the Military Academy. Ironically, it was the Anglo-Egyptian Treaty which opened up the possibility of a military career to Nasser, the son of a post-master. One of the clauses of the Treaty allowed for the 'Egyptianisation' of the army, hitherto the preserve of the Turco-Circassian Ottoman elite. However, Nasser's police file counted heavily against him, and he was turned down by the Academy when he first applied in 1936.

He began a law course at Cairo University, and half-heartedly considered applying to the police college. Finally, he plucked up the courage to approach the Under-Secretary of War, who was in charge of the selection board for the Academy, Ibrahim Khairi Pasha. The minister was either amused or impressed by the intense young man who talked his way into his office to ask for his help. His intervention seems to have made a crucial difference, both to Nasser's life and the course of Egyptian history. Nasser joined the Military Academy in 1937.

Crisis of the old order

4 February 1942: a squadron of British tanks surrounded the Abdin palace in Cairo where King Farouq was conferring with his ministers after receiving an ultimatum from the British ambassador telling him he must appoint a Wafdist government by 6pm that night or 'face the consequences'. The British author-ities suspected that the King and many at court were sympathetic to the advancing German army and were desperate to secure their rear as Rommel's tanks swept through the desert towards El Alamein.

King Farouq

At around 9 p.m., Miles Lampson, the Ambassador, accompanied by a party of British soldiers and General Stone, Commander of British forces in Egypt, forced his way through the palace gates. The Egyptian Royal Guard could only look on helplessly – the King refused them permis-sion to resist. The Ambassador's party burst into the King's study, revolvers drawn, and while Farouq's Albanian guards watched from behind the curtains, Lampson repeat-ed his ultimatum to the young monarch: a government of Britain's choosing or abdication. After a moment's hesitation Farouq agreed.

Out of all the great drama of World War II, it was this one scene – embellished by rumour and hearsay – which played over and over again in the minds of Nasser and his contemporaries. Most of the generation of cadets who joined the Military Academy with Nasser saw 4 February 1942 as a turning point in their lives, and by extension, a turning point in Egyptian history.

Nasser was at this time far from Cairo, having recently returned from the Sudan to a posting in El Alamein, near Alexandria. His reaction to the events of February 1942 was preserved in a letter to an old school friend, Hasan al-Nashar: *I believe the English were playing with only one trump card in their hands. They only wanted to threaten us. If they had felt there were some Egyptians who intended to shed their blood and to oppose force to force, they would have withdrawn like prostitutes ... As for us, as for the army, this event has been a deep shock; hitherto the officers talked only of enjoyment and pleasure. Now they talk of sacrifice and of defending dignity at the cost of their lives ... You see them repenting of not having intervened in spite of their obvious weakness to restore the country's dignity and cleanse its honour in blood. But the future is ours.* [14]

Khaled Mohi-al-Din, an eighteen-year old 2nd Lieutenant in the 1st Tank Regiment remembers a stormy debate at the Officers' Club, immediately after the incident. 'There were about three or four hundred officers passionately discussing what we should do ... there was the idea of a procession to Abdin Palace to voice our rejection of the incident to the King. However, someone mentioned that military discipline forbade officers from taking part in demonstrations or marches. I recall that Ahmad Abd-al-Aziz, a respected officer from whom we had learnt a lot about patriotism at the Military College, stood up and declared that the Royal Guard officer, Ahmad Saleh Husni, had wasted a historic opportunity. He should have shot the British officer; if they had killed him he would have been a martyr, a symbol to Egypt of rejecting and resisting occupation.' [15]

As Nasser raged in his barracks in the desert and the young officers in Cairo argued into the night, General Muhammad

King Farouq inspecting a guard of honour

Naguib – later the public face of the Free Officers' movement and Egypt's first president – sat down to write a letter resigning his commission in protest at the affront to the army and the King.

Ten years later, in July 1952, the same young officers who had raged at Farouq's humiliation at the hands of the British ambassador would hand him a remarkably similar ultimatum of their own: abdicate or face the consequences. What turned their wounded pride to high treason? Between 1942 and 1952 whole sections of the Egyptian state began to crumble under the pressure of the nationalist movement. The cosy arrangement between the palace, the great landlords and the British, which maintained Egypt's social and political order, broke down. The parliamentary parties could not hold back the growing numbers on the streets. Workers' strikes multiplied, spreading out from foreign-owned firms to Egyptian businesses. The loyalty of first the police, and then the army was hollowed out by nationalist agitation in the ranks.

1940: Carrying the flag of his battalion on parade

In place of the chanting, rebellious crowd of schoolboys who joined the protests of 1936, a great social movement emerged. In a period marked by the decay of imperial power, the politics of the street now reached maturity. The most influential currents in Egyptian politics were outside the control of the elite: Communism, radical nationalism and political Islam. The social forces which were the constituency of these newly powerful ideologies were also outside the traditional ruling class: workers, peasants, students, the lower middle classes and young officers – no longer the Turco-Circassian aristocrats of former generations, but the sons of postmasters and clerks.

Of all these currents, the army emerged last and was weaker than the others. The future Free Officers probably did not write their first leaflet until 1949. Their beliefs were an unstable mishmash of ideas. Yet the failure of others to deliver the deathblow to the old regime turned the soldiers into central players, and set Nasser on the road to power.

The price of peace

Economic developments during the war were a powerful motor for social and political discontent. Although ordinary Egyptians felt the pinch of shortages and rising living costs, in many ways the war was good for Egypt's economy. The British Army's insatiable appetite for military supplies encouraged industrial growth and diversification. Everything from army kit to spare parts for vehicles suddenly had to be produced in Egypt as the front lines drew ever closer. Thousands of jobs were created for local workers in the huge British camps. This hothouse economic growth helped to cushion Egyptians for a while from the impact of spiralling prices and rents. The end of hostilities in 1945 brought an abrupt end to some of the conditions which had sustained the wartime boom. Thousands of labourers employed by the British lost their jobs. Egyptian industry, protected throughout much of the war from international competition, was suddenly exposed once again to the ups and downs of the world market.

The first signs of working-class militancy came during the war. In particular, the textile workers of Shubra al-Khayma in Cairo were active in building independent unions after 1942. Strikes over pay, conditions and trade union recognition rapidly became politicised as a result of government repression and British war-time restrictions. By late 1945 the level of industrial unrest was steadily increasing: Shubra was under martial law as wage disputes spiralled into a full-scale confrontation with the government.

Nuqrashi Pasha, the prime minister, dropped the spark which set the nationalist movement alight once again. He wrote to the British government asking for talks on the re-negotiation of the 1936 Treaty. The publication of the prime minister's note and the British reply in February 1946 set thousands of students on a march from the university to the royal palace to demand British withdrawal. When they reached the Abbas Bridge over the Nile, the students were attacked by the British Army and the Egyptian police force. Dozens were shot dead or wounded and others drowned after the authorities opened the bridge under the feet of the marchers. Far from calming the tension, the Abbas Bridge massacre became a rallying cry for the movement, which coalesced around a single, simple slogan: 'British evacuation now!' Student activists joined trade unionists to form the National Committee of Workers and Students (NCWS), which soon had branches nation-wide.

A national day of action, known as 'Evacuation Day', was planned for 21 February. According to the left-wing Wafdist paper, *Al-Wafd al-Misry*, demonstrations and strikes took place in every major town in the Delta and as far south as Assyut. An eyewitness account was sent to the Communist Party of Great Britain on 22 February 1946. 'In the whole of Cairo a complete general strike took place. Shops, cafés, restaurants, cinemas, trains, buses, schools – everything came to a standstill ... students and workers marched together, shouting their slogan 'evacuation of Egypt and the Sudan' ... motorised battalions of the army, patrolling the streets, were acclaimed by the population shouting 'long live the army of the people' ... soldiers and officers of the army were strongly affected by these popular signs of sympathy.'[16]

Army life

During all this ferment, Nasser was living a relatively comfortable and outwardly conventional middle-class existence as an instructor at the Military Academy. His first few years in the army had been uneventful; he kept his outbursts of political passion for letters home to friends or private conversation with his colleagues. After passing his final exams at the Academy in July 1938 he was commissioned 2nd Lieutenant in the infantry and posted to Mankabad, not far from his father's home village of Beni Murr. Anwar Sadat, later Nasser's successor as President and another leading figure in the Free Officers, painted a romantic picture of these first few months of military life. 'One evening in the winter of 1938 we climbed the Jebel Sherif to have dinner together: lentils, chestnuts and sugar cane. Gamal said: "*Let us make this meeting into an historic reunion. Let us take a vow to stay faithful to the friendship, which unites us. This unity will permit us to triumph over all obstacles.*" It was my first real encounter with Gamal. Up to then I had not found him too friendly; he was too taciturn for my taste."[17]

Within six months or so of leaving the Military Academy, Nasser accepted a posting in Khartoum, where he would remain for the next three years. The realities of army life soon took the gloss off the young officers' dreams of reform. In a letter written in August 1941 Nasser told his school friend, Hasan al-Nashar, that he felt isolated and misunderstood. *My fault is to be frank. I know nothing about flattery or deviousness. I don't run after my superiors ... Being the only one, in this milieu, who believes in conscience and fidelity, I am persecuted ... Do you remember our plans of reform which were to be carried out in ten years? Now I think they will need a thousand years.*[18]

Despite these complaints, Nasser's life in the Sudan was not entirely lonely. One friendship cemented during this period was his relationship with Abd-al-Hakim Amer. They were complete opposites in temperament: where Nasser was serious and reserved, Amer was relaxed and open. Their relationship ended in tragedy, with Amer's suicide after the disaster of the 1967 war.

After a brief period back in Egypt, Nasser returned to the Sudan again in September 1942 before securing a job as an instructor in the Military Academy in May 1943. A year later he married Tahia Muhammad Kazim, the 22-year old sister of a friend. They settled in Manshiet al-Bakry, a suburb of Cairo.

May 1940: Nasser in Khartoum, Sudan, holding his pet monkey

Their house, a modest villa on Manshiet al-Tiran Street, was
Nasser's home for the rest of his life. It soon had to accommodate
a growing family: Nasser and Tahia would have five children in
all – three boys and two girls.

Middle-class life shaped Nasser's world view and those of his
closest comrades. Entry into the officer corps gave them secure

and relatively well-paid employment in a society where most lived in poverty and insecurity. Thanks to hire-purchase they could afford some luxuries – cars, refrigerators, record-players – but they were still a world away from the wealth of the old landed elite with their armies of servants and country estates. Nasser, the son of a postmaster, never lost his resentment of those born into wealth and power. The one time he visited the playground of the young rich at the Gezira Sporting Club in Cairo he hated it so much he vowed never to enter the place again. Yet the young officers had as little faith in 'the people' as they did in the elite. Khaled Mohi-al-Din introduced Nasser to two prominent Communist activists, Ahmad Fu'ad and 'Comrade Badr', the secretary-general of the Democratic Movement for National Liberation. Nasser was initially impressed by the two men and asked what they did for a living. Despite hearing that Ahmad Fu'ad was a judge his enthusiasm quickly waned when Mohi-al-Din revealed that Comrade Badr was a mechanic by trade. *'His leader is a mechanic'* he would say, pointing at Mohi-al-Din, when he wanted to score a point in the Free Officers' debates.[19]

The movement grows

Marriage and fatherhood did not end Nasser's political restlessness. In the same year that he married Tahia he had already made contact with activists from different sections of the growing nationalist movement. The network of friends and colleagues, which would later form the core of the Free Officers' movement, was beginning to take shape. But as yet, Nasser and his colleagues had nothing more than shared political sympathies to bind them together. There is little evidence that the Free Officers existed as an organised group until after 1948. It was as individuals that the members of the future military conspiracy were drawn into the periphery of the radical groups of the day. Nasser had extensive contacts with both the Muslim Brotherhood and Communist activists.

Many of the movements which dominated Egyptian politics during the 1940s would have been familiar to Nasser from the protests of his school days in the 1930s. However, in the forties the gap between the established parties, in particular the Wafd, and its more radical opponents widened. This vacuum in official politics allowed opposition groups such as the Communists and the Muslim Brotherhood to gain unprecedented influence. Disillusion with the Wafd was wide-spread and even some Wafdist grandees had become cynical about their own party. In 1943 Makram 'Ubayd, a leading Wafdist, published details of the party's involvement in corruption in his 'Black Book'.[20]

Founded in 1928 in Ismailiyya by the school teacher Hassan al-Banna, the Muslim Brotherhood has played an important role in Egyptian politics ever since. A combination of political party and gigantic welfare organisation, the Brotherhood campaigns to introduce Islamic reforms into the state, and champions Islamic values in society.

The Brotherhood has often found itself in opposition to the government. Under Hassan al-Banna's leadership, the Brotherhood oscillated between the nationalist movement and the Palace. After al-Banna's murder in 1948, his successors first worked closely with Nasser after the revolution of 1952, but then clashed with the Free Officers and were driven underground in 1954.

The Muslim Brotherhood claimed between 500,000 and a million members during the late 1940s. It had a network of branches across the country and an array of social projects, clinics, and schools and produced vast numbers of pamphlets, books and periodicals. The Brotherhood's 'Secret Apparatus', an underground paramilitary body, was accused by the government of organising assassinations and terrorist attacks.

Khaled Mohi-al-Din recalls how he and Nasser were among a number of officers attracted to the Brotherhood towards the end of World War Two. They met with the Brotherhood's Supreme Guide and were even sworn into the Secret

Apparatus in a melodramatic ceremony held in a darkened room.[21] The two officers were quickly disappointed, however. As trained soldiers they knew more about weapons and tactics than their instructors in the Secret Apparatus, and the Brotherhood's sudden rapprochement with the government after 1946 further alienated them.

'I had long discussions with Gamal Abd-al-Nasser about our relationship with the Muslim Brotherhood. He voiced his fears that the Brotherhood was exploiting us, as officers, to serve its own interests and not those of the nation. We acknowledged that we had involved ourselves with the Brotherhood more than was necessary and we should withdraw.'[22]

Communist organisations also found an audience in the nationalist movement. Although they had none of the numerical weight of the Brotherhood, the Communists recruited many leading trade unionists during the forties. Henri Curiel, son of a wealthy Jewish banker, set up the Egyptian Movement for National Liberation (EMNL) in 1943. Hillel Schwartz, another Jew from a similar background to Curiel's, set up Iskra, a propagandist group which attracted a following of intellectuals and students. Iskra joined the EMNL in 1947 to form the Democratic Movement for National Liberation – known as Hadeto from its initials in Arabic.

One of the Communists' weaknesses was their lack of unity. The merger between the EMNL and Iskra fell apart, and the DMNL dissolved into competing factions. For Henri Curiel, the political problems of the period were largely a result of the inexperience of the leading members of the groups. 'At the time it could be said that the masses were still ready to follow us. But we no longer knew where to lead them: we were completely inexperienced. We were not the only ones to realise this. The Prime Minister, Sidqi Pasha, was perfectly well aware of it...'[23]

The protests of 1946 were halted by the arrest of leading activists. However, a year and a half later, a rash of strikes, directed at Egyptian-owned firms as well as foreign enterprises, was sparked off by a dispute in the Misr Spinning mill in Mahalla al-Kubra in September 1947. Male nurses at the Qasr al-Aini Hospital were in a violent strike in April 1948, where police sent in to deal with them were showered with a hail of concrete slabs, boiling water and mattresses, which the nurses set on fire.

A few days before the nurses' dispute, the police had been involved in a national strike of their own. Unlike the confrontations with workers over pay and conditions of the previous months, the police strike was directly political. Mounting pressure from the lower ranks of the police force for an amnesty for all their colleagues who had been disciplined for participating in the nationalist movement brought thousands of officers and policemen out on strike against the government. Troops were called in to direct the traffic and keep order, and in Alexandria a demonstration of police officers and men was joined by workers and students. As the policemen began to drift back to work the following day, rioting broke out in some areas of the city. According to the *Egyptian Gazette*, soldiers had been ordered to shoot looters on sight, and the city was under 'mob-rule'.[24]

Throughout all this turmoil, the army had remained the one force the government could count on to maintain order, despite the influence of nationalist ideas among the officers. Nasser, as an instructor at the Military Academy, did not face the dilemma of his colleagues who were called out time and time again to police demonstrations and strikes. Ahmad Hamroush describes how the officers tried to square military orders to keep the peace with their sympathy for the protestors. 'We didn't support the strikes or take part. But in 1946, for example, we came out with the Army in front of the university to stop the students from demonstrating after the massacre on Abbas Bridge. So we had a meeting and took a decision, even the Muslim Brotherhood officers together with the leftist officers, we took the decision not to open fire on the students, in any circumstances.'[25]

Disillusion in Gaza

It was war in Palestine, which finally set the officers on the road to mutiny. When British forces withdrew from Palestine, in May 1948, the Egyptian government seized the opportunity to turn the attention of nationalist activists onto an external enemy by sending a token number of troops to defend the Palestinians. In reality, the troops mobilized by the Arab League arrived far too late. Since the publication of the UN partition plan in 1947, Zionist militias had already begun to seize areas marked out for the future Palestinian state. Thousands of Palestinians fled the Israeli advance and by the time Egyptian troops arrived at the border, the Gaza Strip was already teeming with refugees.

Nasser, Abd-al-Hakim Amer and a number of their friends volunteered as soon as war broke out in Palestine. When they arrived at the front they found almost everything in chaos. Nasser discovered that no provision had made for hot meals for his troops, instead he was sent off with £1,000 to buy cheese and olives from local farmers. In contrast to Israeli troops, who were supplied with Czech arms, Egyptian soldiers struggled to make do with ancient rifles and unreliable grenades. Both at the front and in Cairo, rumours began to fly that corrupt politicians were making a killing by supplying the Egyptian army with defective arms. Naguib in his memoirs later recalled how 'supply officers, in league with King and his cronies, had been buying sub-standard munitions and pocketing the difference between what they had charged the government and what they had actually paid.'[26]

Meanwhile, the soldiers had little idea why they were fighting. Nasser later recalled that he asked a private in his brigade what he thought was going on. The man replied that they were simply taking part in the 'Rebiki manoeuvres', annual army exercises held in Sinai each year.[27] On another occasion he saw an Egyptian soldier turn and flee from the battlefield. *I said to him: 'why are you running away?' He said: 'In Egypt I don't even have an inch of ground to my name.'*[28]

Nasser (middle) and his comrades during a lull in the fighting for Palestine

General Muhammad Naguib, who earned the nickname 'bullet-proof'[29] during the campaign in Palestine, found many of the same problems. He had to leave field guns behind after reaching the Egyptian railhead because no transport had been provided for them. Meanwhile his troops were desperately short of ammunition.

Nasser was attached as a Staff Major to the 6th Brigade. As the campaign lurched from truce to battle and back to truce again, he experienced with increasing anger the brutality and muddle of war. *I said to myself that humanity does not deserve to live if it does not work with all its strength for peace.* He learnt that one of his friends had been killed. *I swore that if one day, I found myself in a responsible position, I should think a thousand times before sending our soldiers to war. I should only do it if it was absolutely necessary, if the fatherland was threatened, and if nothing could save it but the fire of battle.*[30]

By October, Nasser was at the Fallujah crossroads, where Egyptian forces were encircled by the Israelis. Despite heavy bombardment and fierce Israeli assaults, the Fallujah garrison managed to hold out until the ceasefire of January 1949. Under the armistice agreement, Nasser and his comrades were allowed to march out with their colours flying. They returned changed men, more convinced than ever that their real enemies were at home.

The war also showed the nationalist opposition in a new light to the young officers. Despite their misgivings about the autocratic nature of some of the major opposition groups, such as the Muslim Brotherhood, the officers had seen how the volunteer irregulars fought bravely in the campaign. The Muslim Brotherhood in particular had organised units of fighters from among students and workers. Every day for several weeks the Brotherhood's newspaper, *al-Ikhwan al-Muslimeen,* printed front-page reports of the young men who had died a martyr's death in Palestine.

The Free Officers emerge

Not long after the end of the war, Nasser and a handful of close friends began to meet regularly to discuss the way forward. According to Khaled Mohi-al-Din, there were five at the first meeting: Nasser, Abd-al-Muni'm Abd-al-Ra'uf, Kamal-al-Din Hussein, who were both close the Muslim Brotherhood, Hasan Ibrahim, and himself. Nasser also added the name of his close friend, Abd-al-Hakim Amer. At first the discussion ranged over the grievances of the nationalist movement – the weak governments, the corruption of the King, the arrogance of the British. But the experience of war in Palestine had thrown these questions into sharper relief. Nasser asked his colleagues, *if we were defeated by groups of Israeli volunteers, how shall we face the British? How shall we liberate the country?* [31]

Nasser had other reasons for seeking the support of his friends. In June 1949, he was summoned before the Prime Minister, Isma'il Abd-al-Hadi. An army manual with his name in the flyleaf had been seized by police during a raid on the Muslim Brotherhood's Secret Apparatus. Here was concrete proof of a link between the officer corps and the government's opponents. Nasser talked his way out of the situation, but after this narrow escape he was left in no doubt that the opportunities for individual political activism would be sharply curtailed.

The small group which met in Nasser's living room was soon able to recruit like-minded officers. At first their ideas were vague: to uphold the honour of the army and to liberate Egypt. The first leaflet, which was issued in 1949 or 1950, discussed the issue of the defective weapons used in the Palestine war. The 'Free Officers' was now the signature of an underground network. The conspirators pooled money to buy a duplicating machine for eighty pounds to enable a more efficient distribution of leaflets.

Gradually the new organisation began to take shape. The original core of the Free Officers became a Command Committee. A cell structure was created so that only leading members knew the names of the group's members. Nasser was cautious about committing the Free Officers to a specific political programme, however. When Khaled Mohi-al-Din wrote up a lengthy list of objectives for the group, Nasser and most of the other Command Committee members were sceptical and encouraged him to put it aside.

In a period marked by the decay of Egypt's mainstream nationalist movement, the Wafd, it was not surprising that the Free Officers shunned the established political parties. But Nasser also insisted that members of other opposition organisations, whether Communists or Muslim Brothers, could only join the Free Officers as individuals, and not as representatives of a group. Some of this scepticism probably had its roots in the officers' experience of working with the Brotherhood and the Communists. However, it also reflected their belief that all political parties carried with them the seeds of their own corruption. As Nasser used to say, *when I hear the word 'organisation', I draw my sword.*[32] In Nasser's case, Tawfiq al-Hakim's writings, which he read avidly as a teenager, may also have been influential. Al-Hakim held that intellectuals should keep aloof from political parties, a rule that he practised himself.

For the young officers, the counterbalance to the degeneration of civilian nationalist politics was not more, or different parties, but the army itself, the bearer of a purified nationalism. Later, Nasser would broaden his perspective to expand the role of the vanguard to the state as a whole, but his suspicion of party organisation remained intact.

The Officers' Club elections

By autumn 1951 the nationalist movement had begun to revive, pushing the Wafd into abrogating the 1936 Treaty with Britain on 8 October. This was the signal for further protests and strikes. Sugar refinery workers went on strike over the rising cost of living. Other groups of workers soon followed, forcing the government to step in and settle the dispute by paying a cost of living allowance. Guerrilla war broke out in the Canal Zone between bands of volunteer fighters, the fedayeen, and the British Army. Various opposition groups from the Muslim Brotherhood to the Communists began to raise units of volunteers. They launched a series of attacks on British positions to which the British responded by occupying Port Said, Ismailiyya and Suez. At the same time the strikes continued to gather momentum. Workers from the Canal Zone quit their jobs in a general boycott of foreign companies and forced the Wafd into promising work for the unemployed in Cairo. In Ismailiyya elementary schools went on strike as the school-children organised their own protests against British occupation. Transport workers in the major cities walked out, demanding better pay and the nationalisation of the public transport system. Textile workers also took action and the government had to intervene to end a national strike by pharmacy workers.

It was in this context that the Free Officers took the decision to put forward candidates for the Board of the Officers' Club. In place of the Palace favourites who usually topped the nominations, the Free Officers asked General Muhammad Naguib to stand. Abd-al-Hakim Amer introduced Nasser to the general, who was smarting from a slight at the hands of the palace: he had been passed over for promotion. Naguib later recalled, 'it was a strange reversal of roles for a senior officer to be examined, however respectfully, by two of his juniors, but I was not displeased. I was coming to the conclusion that Egypt's salvation depended on its junior officers.'[33]

The Free Officers defeated the King's candidates, marking a new phase in the group's development. They were the talk of the barracks, and could now count on a substantial network of supporters, but they were more exposed than ever before. The humiliation of the King's supporters in the Officers' Club elections brought the officers into direct confrontation with the Palace.

The day Cairo burned

In January 1952 fighting in the Canal Zone reached a new level of intensity. The fedayeen launched an attack on the British base at Tel al-Kabir. In retaliation the British chose to attack the auxiliary police force, which was an easier target than the mobile guerrilla units. The police station in Ismailiyya was besieged by British forces on 25 January and 46 policemen were killed.

The following day, Saturday 26 January, went down in history as 'Black Saturday'. Thousands of people spilled into the streets of Cairo to join protests by striking policemen. As students poured over the bridge from the university in Gizeh a crowd assembled in front of the Cabinet offices, bringing Abd-al-Fattah Hasan, Minister for Social Affairs, to the balcony. Jean and Simonne Lacouture, two French journalists, described the scene:

'Thick-set and dark, with a glint in his eyes and his tarboosh at a jaunty angle, Abdul Fattah Hasan addressed the demonstrators: "this is your day! You will be avenged! And we will expose ourselves to the enemy's fire, in the front rank!" But as a professional lawyer he was quick to grasp that he had no control over this mass of people.'[34]

Policemen standing with their arms round the shoulders of the students shouted back at him. Young officers sat watching in mocking amusement. Meanwhile the street continued to fill, and cries from the back of crowd demanded arms from the Russians to fight for the Canal.

'It was surely not by chance that the mass of listeners, unsatisfied by the Minister's long and brilliant denunciation of the British, the purpose of which was clearly to gain time and calm the mob, produced a list of the "People's demands". They called for an absolute boycott of the British; the despatch of armed forces to the Canal, and a treaty of friendship with the Soviet Union. Thus, like some Popular Front meeting, the dialogue between the minister and the crowd went on for almost three hours.' [35]

Meanwhile, elsewhere in the city, the anger turned to rage and fire. Flames consumed a cinema, singeing the billboards for the latest film: 'When Worlds Collide'. The crowds passed on to Shepheard's Hotel, Barclay's Bank and Chrysler's, before making for King Farouq's favourite night spots and setting the Turf Club alight. All across Cairo, symbols of royal wealth and colonial power would be charred wrecks before the day was through.

January 1952: the Shepheard's Hotel after the Cairo fire

The Army moves

Despite the devastation, the old regime limped on. None of the opposition movements was strong or willing enough to take its place. The Communist groups were too small, and in any case they pinned their hopes for change on mobilising a broad alliance of nationalist forces, so would not move on their own. The Muslim Brotherhood's conservative leadership had temporarily drawn close to the King. The Wafd had lost control of events. By January 1952 the party was tailing rather than leading the nationalist movement.

The King managed to dissolve the government and dismiss the Wafdist prime minister, Mustafa Nahhas Pasha, on 27 January. Ali Maher formed a new government, which only survived until 1 March. The new government, headed by Naguib Hilali, attempted to secure its position with pay rises for the police and army and postponed the elections. Hilali's cabinet lasted until 28 June, before following its predecessors and resigning. The third government since January took office four days later with the King's press advisor as a member of the cabinet.

The months following Black Saturday were also filled with uncertainty and tension for the Free Officers. Nasser uncharacteristically broke with the discipline of the group to organise an attempt on the life of Hussein Sirri Amer, the commander of the frontier corps and a supporter of the King. He later described how the failed assassination was a turning point. He realised that solving Egypt's problems could not be achieved simply by killing a handful of unpopular courtiers. *I got home and lay down in bed, my mind in a fever ... All night long I could not sleep. I lay on my bed in the darkness lighting one cigarette after another. ... 'Our method must change. This is not the positive action we should aim for. The problem is more dangerous and deeply rooted.'*[36]

The assassination attempt led to a confrontation with other members of the Free Officers' leadership: Salah Salem of the artillery and Abd-al-Latif al-Bughdadi, an Air Force officer, were furious at the risks that Nasser had taken. Despite the tension, Nasser was elected Chairman of the officers' Command Committee.

The final countdown to the overthrow of the old order began mid-way through July. In an attempt to crush the opposition in the army, the King dissolved the board of the Officers' Club on 16 July and threatened to place dissenters under arrest. A meeting of the Command Committee agreed a date to seize control of the army. The officers settled on the night of August 2/3. Events moved faster than they anticipated. On 19 July Muhammad Naguib heard from one of the cabinet ministers that the government had a list of the leaders of the Free Officers and was planning to arrest them. At the same time news leaked out that a new cabinet was being formed with the officers' enemy Hussein Sirri Amer as Minister of War.

The Free Officers' plans were brought forward to the night of 22/23 July. With the troops under their command they would seize the key areas of the capital and arrest the general staff, before removing the King. After a final meeting at Khaled Mohi-al-Din's house that afternoon, the members of Command Committee left to prepare for zero hour. Nasser contacted the Muslim Brotherhood and the DMNL to ask for their support. Anwar Sadat went to the cinema. Khaled Mohi-al-Din spent the evening with his wife and children.

Late that evening word of the planned coup reached the palace. An emergency meeting of army commanders – with the pointed exception of Muhammad Naguib – was convened at army head-quarters near the Qubba Bridge. The Free Officers' carefully constructed plan hung by a thread. Nasser and Amer changed into civilian clothes and sped off in Nasser's little black Austin, hoping to gather forces to arrest the commanders before they could gain the barracks and take control of the troops. As they drew near to the Qubba Bridge they heard the rumble of artillery and saw a battalion approaching. Suspicious of their intentions, the soldiers put them under arrest. Just as all seemed lost, the battalion's commanding officer appeared – the two conspirators were delighted to see the face of a fellow Free Officer, Yusuf Siddiq, who had moved his troops out early from Hikestep in the suburbs of Cairo.

Yusuf Siddiq's battalion took the headquarters building and arrested the chief of staff. Meanwhile the Free Officers' columns were finally moving into place. The commanders who had left the meeting at headquarters were arrested one-by-one. Khaled Mohial-Din was hailed by one senior officer who tried to walk through his unit to get to the barracks: "'Please give me a car to take me to the corps, because there is a mutiny!' I smiled and said, "Sorry – we are the mutiny.'" [37] By 6 a.m. the mutineers had taken control of the skies as well, as Air Force units loyal to the Free Officers' cause took off from the airfields around Cairo. Waking up on the morning of 23 July, Egyptians turned on the radio to hear the voice of Anwar Sadat, reading a proclamation in the name of Muhammad Naguib announcing the coup to the world.

An unlikely revolution

'As I came out of the broadcasting station and drove up to our headquarters in the north of Cairo, I saw the streets of the metropolis crowded with people as I had never seen them before. Men, old and young, women and children, were kissing each other, shaking hands, coming together in small clusters or large circles – but all the time in total silence.' [38]

Anwar Sadat's recollections of the morning of the coup encapsulate the Free Officers' myth of their revolution. A new Egypt was born on 23 July 1952, with the army acting as the agent of change. The Egyptian people, in whose name Nasser would later reap the whirlwind of Great Power politics, could only watch in passive, silent approval.

The reality was different. The early years of the new regime –not even a republic until 1953 – were full of conflict. The Free Officers struck the final blow against the monarchy, but they succeeded because the foundations of state had been undermined by others. The students, textile workers, tram drivers, government clerks and policemen who joined Egypt's movement for national liberation had all played their part in this process. Yet when the government was paralysed, the movement's leaders hesitated and retreated, setting the stage for the Free Officers' entrance. Despite this, it was no easy matter to 'turn off' the protests and strikes after July 1952. The Nasser of this period was not the idol of later years. He was seen by many as a sinister power behind the scenes: a schemer and autocrat. It was his rival, General Muhammad Naguib, who won the adoration of the crowd.

Born in Sudan in 1901 (c.1901-84), Muhammad Naguib was chosen by the Free Officers to be the public face of the revolution. As a senior officer in a hierarchical military world his presence added weight to their project.

He became Prime Minister of Egypt in September 1952, and President the following year. After clashing with Nasser in 1954 he was dismissed and placed under house arrest for many years. He died in 1984.

As the officers' government hit out first at the trade unions and the Communists, and then moved against the Muslim Brothers, many thought the return of the old regime only a matter of time. However, both the Brotherhood and the Communists underestimated the resilience of the new regime, and of Nasser in particular. It was not some obscure chemistry of Nasser's charisma which worked this change, rather, it was the practical steps taken by the officers to build a constituency for their rule which set the stage for Nasser's victory. Even having created a social base for the new regime, Nasser still had no guarantee of success; division and confusion among his opponents were the final element in his victory.

Who called the tune in the revolution?

News of the Free Officers' success was greeted enthusiastically by most Egyptians. However for both the Communists and the Muslim Brothers, more was at stake. Both currents had taken the risky step of cultivating contacts inside the armed forces. Both had their partisans among the Free Officers' network. Communist presses had printed Free Officers' leaflets, while the Muslim Brothers knew leading members of the army group as comrades-in-arms from the siege of Fallujah to the battle for the Canal.

Nasser embodied this contradictory relationship perfectly. Before the coup, Nasser collected leaflets printed for the officers by the DMNL's secret printing press in person. The printer, who knew the young man who came to take the leaflets only as

Muhammad Naguib (c. 1901-84): in September 1952 he became
Prime Minister, and President a year later.

'Maurice', was surprised to see his face on the front page of the newspapers in the days following the revolution in July 1952. His joy was short-lived, however; he and the other workers on the DMNL's printing press were arrested shortly afterwards. [39]

At the same time, Nasser cultivated strong personal relations with leading figures in the Brotherhood, including Abd-al-Rahman al-Sanadi, head of the Brotherhood's underground para-military wing, the Secret Apparatus. Before the coup a detailed plan of action was agreed between key figures in the Brotherhood and leaders of the Free Officers. The Brotherhood would mobilize to fill the streets at the first sign of opposition, with the organisation's trained volunteers acting as a kind of civil defence force, to protect places of worship and public buildings.

Both the Brotherhood and the Communists were soon to be disillusioned. Within two years the Free Officers drove the Communists underground and sent the leaders of the Brotherhood to the gallows.

The end of King Farouq

The first dilemma which confronted the Free Officers was the fate of King Farouq. By 1952, the prince whose accession to the throne in 1936 encouraged hopes of reform was a potent symbol of the decay of the old order. The royal palace was a by-word for intrigue and corruption. Any loyalty which the officers felt towards the King in 1942 at the time of his confrontation with the British army had long since evaporated. The palace was blamed for the Egyptian army's catastrophic intervention in the war in Palestine, and in particular for the scandal of the troops' defective weapons. Many officers also felt that the King and his favourites were med-dling in the army's affairs. For the Free Officers this was about more than thwarted ambition and blocked promotions: they had just come out on top after a six-month battle of nerves with the palace. Indecision now could endanger them all.

It quickly became clear that Farouq was isolated. Reports from the outlying garrisons flooded into the officers' headquarters: Rafah and Al-Arish on the border with the Gaza Strip declared for the revolution, followed quickly by Suez. Most important of all, word reached Cairo that the troops in Alexandria, Farouq's last line of defence, were under the control of the Free Officers. After a brief meeting on July 24 the officers agreed to send a delegation to Alexandria to depose the King.

On the evening of July 25 a sudden crisis erupted. Wing Commander Gamal Salem, who had been sent to Alexandria with Naguib, flew back to Cairo with a proposal that the King be tried and executed. According to Naguib's account, after failing to convince his colleagues in Alexandria, Gamal Salem hoped to win the backing of Nasser and the other members of the Free Officers' leadership. He returned a few hours later with Nasser's answer: *Let us spare Farouq and send him into exile. History will sentence him to death.* [40]

The expulsion of the King took place as planned. Farouq, accompanied by his family and 204 pieces of luggage, sailed into the sunset on his luxury yacht, the Mahrussa. Naguib later recalled the awkward moment when he bade Farouq farewell. He agonised over whether to address the King as 'Your majesty', settling in the end for 'Effendim' – 'Sir'. "'We were loyal to the

King Farouq (1920-65) was seen by many Egyptians as a corrupt playboy, whose court favourites were hated but often feared. His 1951 marriage to Narriman Sadiq, a glamorous commoner, was meant to revive affection for the monarchy. Although the royal couple produced a son, Ahmad Fu'ad, it was only months later that the Free Officers took power and unceremoniously deposed King Farouq.

A year later, Free Officers finished off the monarchy for good, converting Farouq's palaces into museums or state buildings and auctioning off his prized collection of rare coins. Narriman, who spent little more than a year as queen, divorced Farouq not long after.

23 July 1952: troops outside Abdin Palace, Cairo

throne in 1942 but many things have changed since then." "Yes I know. Many things have changed." "It was you, effendim, who forced us to do what we have done."' [41]

After the coup

Naguib's embarrassment in front of King Farouq was a symptom of the officers' uncertainty over their new role. Once in power the Free Officers had to act quickly to secure their precarious position. They agreed to ask Ali Maher, a former prime minister, to head an interim government. There was a slight delay when the Command Committee realised no-one actually had his address, and Anwar Sadat had to be sent off to look for him with the help of a journalist.

Meanwhile, among the Free Officers themselves realignments were taking place. New faces were added to the original core. Disputes emerged over the direction of the revolution. The abdication of the King raised a constitutional problem. The leadership of the Free Officers was told by legal experts that a Regency Council would have to be formed to rule in the name of Farouq's infant son, thus requiring the recall of parliament and new elections within two months. A heated debate took place, at which Nasser argued strongly in favour of holding elections and found himself alone. He promptly submitted his resignation as Chairman of the Free Officers Command Council, which had replaced the group's old Command Committee shortly after the coup, and went home. Within hours the Command Council had decided to ask him to return. In Anwar Sadat's description of the meeting, Nasser's defence of 'democracy' was something of a sham: he wanted merely to underline his authority over his colleagues. 'At dawn Nasser came back. He had won, by our consent and authorisation. However controversial it may be, that was a historic decision.'[42]

Despite this particular victory, during the first few months in power Nasser was only one member of the Free Officers' collective leadership. Over the months that followed, he strengthened his position through determination and hard work, but could still find himself in a minority when the Command Council put decisions to a vote.

On his return, Nasser agreed to the formation of the Regency Council without the recall of parliament. When Khaled Mohi-al-Din asked him why he had abandoned his previous position, Nasser argued that a retreat was necessary. *Remember we have problems, Rashad Mahanna is beginning to regroup the artillery behind him. Furthermore, 'Abd al-Mun'im Amin (also from the artillery) is still new and unreliable. So I thought it best to retreat in order to recover our hold over the situation.*[43] The formation of the Regency Council provided an opportunity for Nasser to neutralise Rashad Mahanna, an ambitious officer who had brought the artillery regiments into the coup on 23 July. He was appointed a minister and then a member of the Regency Council. Khaled Mohi-al-Din recalls in his memoirs: 'How grateful he was, and with tears in his eyes thanked us profusely. However, this gratitude did not last long as he realized that we had shelved him to a post of no real worth or value.'[44] Within a few months he had been arrested along with other officers and accused of plotting a coup over the Free Officers' plans to drop a clause from the constitution designating Islam as the state religion.

As these manoeuvres took place, rumours spread among journalists, politicians and diplomats of a secret military junta, which met in King Farouq's old boathouse on the Nile. This was the Command Council, which would later be given a formal role in the state, and renamed the Revolution Command Council (RCC). But despite their shock at the King's abdication, the politicians still felt confident that the soldiers would soon return to their barracks. This view was encouraged by the officers. In his pamphlet, 'The Philosophy of the Revolution', Nasser declared that the army would not remain indefinitely in power. *Our role is that of a guardian only, no more and no less, a guardian for a definite period with a time limit.*[45] In an interview with *Al-Ahram* in June 1953 he explained what the Free Officers had hoped to achieve. *What we all wanted was to purge the army, rid the country of foreign occupation and establish a clean, fair government which would work sincerely for the good of the people. Once in power, we found ourselves faced with the difficult problem of establishing a political, social and economic programme. It was necessary to improvise. We did our best. The divergence of political ideas then obliged us to separate from those who did not agree to apply the majority decisions of the Council of the Revolution and then those of the Government we set up*[46]

A balancing act

Over the summer, the Free Officers' vague political ideas began to take concrete form. They demanded that the existing parties remove from positions of authority those figures most closely associated with the old regime. Even so, it was hard to shake the habit of deference. To underline the transition to a new political era, the officers abolished formal titles. Naguib began levying

The Free Officers: Naguib is seated in the middle of the sofa, between Nasser (on his right) and Amer. Sadat is seated on the far right of the picture.

fines of a piastre on people who called him 'Bey', a Turkish title meaning 'my Lord', only to have to pay a fine himself after referring to Ali Maher as 'His Excellency'. At the same time the Free Officers attempted to reassure foreign investors that the new regime's crusade against the privileges of the old elite was not the precursor of a left-wing programme directed at Egyptian businesses. A law restricting the foreign ownership of Egyptian corporations to 49 percent was changed to allow foreign investors a 51 percent stake.

In August a wave of strikes in Alexandria was suppressed by the police. Textile workers at Kafr al-Dawwar on the outskirts of the city occupied their mill, demanding a freely elected union, the dismissal of abusive supervisors and wage increases. Shots were fired during a demonstration by the striking workers and two soldiers, one policeman and four workers were killed. The Free Officers saw in the strike a challenge to their authority and reacted accordingly. Over 500 workers were arrested, and two, Mustafa Khamis and Muhammad al-Baqari, were given a summary trial at an open-air court and condemned to hang.

When the death sentences were debated by the leading Free Officers, Nasser, along with the two left-wing officers Khaled Mohi-al-Din and Yusuf Siddiq, voted against. However, he later recalled the officers' fury at what they saw as a deliberate attempt to smear the new regime. *The revolution took place on 23 July. The King left on 26 July. In the first week of August, people began to attack this revolution in the name of Communism. There wasn't a single soul in the country who knew who was behind the revolution, but the Communists, or people who call themselves Communists, put out leaflets in the first week of August saying 'this revolution supports colonialism' and 'this revolution is working for the benefit of colonialism'. Of course they didn't have a clue who was behind the revolution in order to make this decision.* [47]

The ferocity of the new regime's response disorientated the left. In Alexandria, tens of thousands of textile workers took strike action and demonstrated. [48] But the biggest Communist group, the DMNL, remained with the government, responding to the repression with muted protest at the hangings while at the same time suggesting the trouble had been caused by 'imperialist agents'. [49] The DMNL paper *Al-Malayin* for 10 September 1952, three days after Khamis and al-Baqari's execution, ran a lead article entitled 'The road of the people and the army - a national front against imperialism and traitors.' [50]

In the long term it was not repression but incorporation which proved a more effective method of taming the trade union movement. Workers were given basic rights at work. In the place of the independent unions founded during the 1940s and led by the left, the Free Officers encouraged the growth of new unions. Hundreds of activists were already in jail by this time, which meant that supporters of the government quickly came to dominate the new leadership. [51]

In addition, the confusion on the left aided the military government. During the first few months of the new regime, several Communist groups shifted towards opposition to the Free Officers. In part this was motivated by the experience of repression and the hangings of Khamis and al-Baqari. But the attitude of the USSR was also crucial. After a period of hesitation, the Soviet press began to attack the Free Officers, and Egyptian Communists were told to break all ties with the soldiers' movement. Opponents of the DMNL intensified their attacks on the organisation, while the DMNL itself was rent with internal dissension. Ahmad Hamroush, a member of the DMNL who was also an activist in the Free Officers, remembers that he and other left-wing colleagues in the Free Officers were bewildered by the government's attacks on the left. As far as they were concerned, the Free Officers and the DMNL were all part of the same movement against imperialism. [52]

Land Reform, 1952: Nasser handing out deeds to *fellahin*

Liquidating feudalism

The land reforms of September 1952 marked a turning point. For the Free Officers as a group, it was the first step towards building an independent political base for themselves. The proposals underscored the difference between the new regime and the failures of the old politicians, who had debated land reform but never carried it out. Prime Minister Ali Maher's attempts to restrict the scope of the law was one factor in the conflict which led to his resignation and the soldiers' entry into the government. Naguib became prime minister in his place, heading a mixed civilian-military cabinet. Nasser was not a member of the new government; his official role at this stage was head of Naguib's personal staff.

At a superficial level, the land reform programme appeared a radical break with the past. The officers' slogan – 'the eradication of feudalism' – conjured up images of soviet-style collectivisation of agriculture. In reality, however, land reform continued the Free Officers' balancing act. It proved that there was more to their rhetoric of social justice than mere slogans – at a time when the new regime was hanging strikers as a warning to the trade unions. Another aim of the reforms was to unlock some of the wealth tied up in the great estates by encouraging landlords to invest in industry.

So the Marxist writer Ahmad Fu'ad and Rashid al-Barawy, who translated Marx's *Das Kapital* into Arabic, had a hand in drafting the law, which was also shaped by the advice of American diplomats. For the Free Officers themselves, it was Gamal Salem, seen by most as a liberal on matters of economic policy, who oversaw the reform process. In economic and social terms, the changes were modest. Only 10 percent of Egypt's cultivable land was targeted for redistribution. Landowners were able to retain up to 300 feddans (approximately 300 acres), while those expropriated received compensation.

Rapid population growth increased the pressure for reform. By the 1950s, around 16 million people out of Egypt's total population of 22 million were dependent on agriculture. These 16 millions had to be supported by a mere 6 million acres of cultivated land, a tall order even given the fertility of Egyptian soils, since improvements in crop yields were barely keeping pace with population increase. Between 1897 and 1949, Egypt's cultivated area rose by 14 percent and crop area increased by 37 percent, but the population doubled.

Despite the growing importance of industry, Egyptian society in the 1940s was still predominately rural. Three-quarters of the population lived in the countryside. Large landowners dominated the rural economy. Makram 'Ubayd, Finance Minister in 1945, described the situation like this: 'Large landowners who own 50 feddans and above comprise 0.5 percent of landowners [but own] 36.9 percent of total landed property, in other words, one-third of the revenue of agricultural land goes to large landowners while the remaining revenue is distributed to 99.5 percent of landowners.'[53]

At an economic level, Egyptian agriculture was anything but feudal. It was highly capitalized, mechanized and well-integrated into the world economy. At a social and political level, the officers' campaign against 'feudalism' struck a chord with millions of Egyptians. As a contemporary observer noted: 'when an Egyptian economist was asked what he meant by a feudal estate, he replied "It means that the landowner keeps a private army to defend his house and his person; and that armed men stand guard over the crops."'[54]

These landowners not only acted as a law unto themselves in the countryside, many had wielded great influence in parliament and in the governments of the 1940s. Two parliamentary bills proposing a limit on the size of landholdings were heavily defeated in 1945 and 1950. Supporters of land reform had few allies in parliament or at the royal court. The Wafd had come more and more to represent the interests of large landowners, while the royal family held the biggest estates in Egypt. As a measure targeting these two groups, the land reform was a very precise instrument of political power. The reform targeted the apex of the old elite, without signalling a general assault on the whole ruling class. One third of the total expropriations took place in estates belonging to the royal family. Altogether 15 to 20 families made up the majority of those expropriated.

The Free Officers took every opportunity to highlight the contrast between the 'feudalist' landowners and the peasant farmers in their smock-like galabiyyahs, who appeared in dozens of press photographs and newsreels, beaming from ear to ear, as the bluff, affable figure of General Naguib handed over title deeds to the land they had tilled for generations.

The Brotherhood

The formation of Naguib's first cabinet marked a new phase in the Free Officers' relations with the Muslim Brotherhood. Individual relationships between members of the Free Officers' group and the Brotherhood went back a long way. Anwar Sadat had worked closely with members of the Brotherhood for years before the Free Officers came together as a coherent group. Nasser himself met Muhammad Labib, who was charged by the Brotherhood with interviewing possible sympathisers in the army, as early as 1944. He and other officers had helped the Brotherhood train volunteers for guerrilla warfare in the Canal Zone.

Both this shared history, and the immediate actions of the new government, seemed to give the Muslim Brotherhood's leaders grounds for optimism about the new regime. After a brief period of hesitation, the Brotherhood's leaders on the Shura Council hailed the success of the officers 'blessed movement'. Abd-al-Rahman al-Banna, father of the Brotherhood's murdered leader Hassan al-Banna, called on the society to 'embrace Naguib and help him with your hearts, your blood, and your wealth.'[55] Meanwhile key supporters of the Brotherhood, such as Abd-al-Mun'im Abd-al-Ra'uf and Rashad Muhanna, were initially appointed to positions of influence. In addition, the Free Officers promised a new investigation into the assassination of Hassan al-Banna, and released members of the Brotherhood jailed by the old regime. The Free Officers' attacks on the left won the support of the Brotherhood's leadership, which had long been enthusiastically anti-Communist. Leading figures in the Brotherhood, including the former literary critic Sayyid Qutb helped draw up policies to curb the activities of the Left in the trade unions and restrict workers' rights.

Yet despite cordial relations on the surface, 'from the very beginning, basic conflict marked the inner private relationship of the Society to the "blessed movement".'[56] The most fundamental contradiction between the Brotherhood and the Free Officers lay in their opposing views of how the new state and society should be built. The Brotherhood wanted an Islamic constitution to reshape the state. The Command Council disagreed, and sacked Rashad Muhanna on 14 October after he continued to argue for it. And when it came to the question of land reform – a key plank of the Free Officers' strategy to build a constituency for the new regime – the Brotherhood's General Guide, Hasan al-Hodeiby, came out in favour of the moderate proposals of Prime Minister Ali Maher. This did not stop Nasser lobbying for the inclusion of Muslim Brotherhood members in the cabinet formed by Naguib after the fall of Ali Maher's government. However, despite the General Guide's initial agreement, the Brotherhood's Shura Council rejected the idea of participation, earning Hasan al-Hodeiby Nasser's lasting resentment.

Behind the scenes

During the first months following the officers' revolution, Nasser did not seek a public role for himself. When his speeches were published as a seven volume set in 1959, only one public meeting from 1952 was featured. Although he appeared alongside his colleagues at public events, to most Egyptians he was just another unknown face among the gaggle of young officers who shadowed General Naguib's footsteps. A picture caption in Naguib's account of his brief season in power provides a revealing comment on this relationship: Naguib is shown emerging from a building followed by Nasser and a group of his colleagues. The text only names the General, however, adding that he is 'accompanied by members of his staff'.[57]

Diplomats, journalists and spies – in other words those who were more deeply concerned with the power structures of the new regime – gradually swung into Nasser's orbit, however. The CIA sent one its most experienced agents, Kermit Roosevelt, to Cairo in October 1952 to establish personal contact. Around the same time articles began to appear in *Rose al-Youssef* naming Nasser as the power behind the scenes in Cairo. *The Times* correspondent was quick to pick up *Rose al-Youssef*'s signals, reporting to readers back in Britain: 'The newspaper adds that the Colonel, in spite of his denials, was the engineer of the Army movement, possesses extreme patience, coolness, and intelligence, and enjoys the confidence of army officers'.[58]

While there was clearly an element of calculation in Nasser's modesty in front the press, his reluctance to claim public credit for the officers' success also reflects his relationship with his fellow Free Officers. Jean Lacouture argues that at this stage Nasser was 'respected by his friends and considered a rank-and-file leader, not a "boss".... He was influential rather than imposing. He argued and tried to persuade, disregarding his rank and privilege. *Primus inter pares*.'[59]

Revolution from above: the Liberation Rally

The first year of the new order saw the Free Officers evolve a new concept of their role in the state. Nasser's account describes vividly how in July 1952 the conspirators seized power as the advance guard of a popular movement against colonial occupation and the monarchy. Transformed into the state's temporary guardians, the officers kept looking over their shoulders, waiting for the arrival of 'the masses'. *I imagined that our role was act as the vanguard, that this role would not last more than a few hours before the masses appeared behind us, marching in serried ranks to the great goal . . . the vanguard performed its task, it stormed the ramparts of tyranny, ousted the tyrant and stood by . . . it waited and waited. Endless crowds appeared, but how different reality is to the imagination: these multitudes were the scattered stragglers from a defeated army.*[60]

In reality, the Free Officers were engaged in a battle for control of the organisations which had provided the backbone of the popular movement of the 1940s: the trade unions, the opposition parties, the student unions. One reason that 'the people' never caught up with the military vanguard was that in order to consolidate their own power, the officers themselves systematically undermined these institutions by destroying their ability to mobilise independently of the state. Nasser played a key role in this process as he led the efforts to create a new, top-down mechanism for mobilising the people behind the army's still-ambiguous revolutionary project: the Liberation Rally. In October 1952, student unions were abolished, leading to clashes between left-wing and nationalist students who opposed the move and members of the Brotherhood's student groups who supported it. Independent trade union leaders were arrested, and supporters of the new government elected in their place. And in January 1953, all political parties were dissolved, with one exception: the Brotherhood.

In the place of the political parties, which the officers argued were tainted by the corruption of the old regime, the government sponsored the creation of the Liberation Rally, an official mass movement, which had Nasser as its secretary-general. The Rally was officially conceived as a replacement for political parties during a 'transitional period' of military rule. Created from above, it had no real life of its own, although Nasser later found it a useful mechanism for giving the appearance of mass mobilisation in support of continued military rule during his conflict with Naguib in March 1954.

The Liberation Rally also gave Nasser an official public role. At the opening of the Rally's offices in Shubin al-Kum on 23 February

1953 he laid out the achievements of the officers' revolution. Before July 1952 *there was social injustice, embodied in the abominable nightmare of feudalism. We inherited a class of rulers and nobles who looked down on the people ... They split the country into two factions, each hating the other even though they were from one class: a camp of slaves, and a caste of masters. We also saw political tyranny, embodied in the two great ogres: foreign occupation and a reckless monarchy.*[61] This divided Egypt belonged the past, he said. In place of conflict, the Liberation Rally promised 'unity, discipline and work'.[62]

In June 1953, the Free Officers marked another milestone: the formal abolition of the monarchy. Nasser entered the cabinet for the first time, as Minister of the Interior and Deputy Prime Minister, while his close friend Abd-al-Hakim Amer took over control of the armed forces from Naguib.

Liberation Rally: Amer at the microphone. The tension between Nasser and Naguib, seated behind him, is already visible on their faces.

By January 1954, Nasser was admitting openly that he had no intention of allowing the restoration of parliamentary government, even if negotiations with the British brought the withdrawal of foreign troops. He told Jean Lacouture, *No, it wouldn't make any sense. In a year and a half we have been able to wipe out corruption. If the right to vote were now restored, the same landowners would be elected – the feudal interests. We don't want the capitalists and the wealthy back in power. If we open the government to them now, the revolution might just as well be forgotten.*[63]

The contest with Naguib

March 1954, not July 1952, marked the real turning point in Egypt's unlikely revolution. It was in March 1954, that Nasser was able to break with the past, and finally out-manoeuvre his opponents. The conflict crystallized around the personality clash between Muhammad Naguib and Nasser, but its roots went much deeper. So it was that Naguib became a symbol for those calling for a return to parliamentary life, while Nasser mobilized the support he had been building over the previous two years to ensure the continuation of military rule.

At a personal level, the conflict between Nasser and Naguib can be explained as a clash between the revolution's leading man and its director. Nasser had no detailed plans for the new society he wanted to create, but he had a strong sense that Egypt had to be transformed in the process. It was big, vague, ideas which gave him his initial sense of purpose: *unity, discipline, work.*[64] Naguib, however, appears to have envisaged merely shifting around the scenery on the political stage. Their choice of words set them apart: Naguib described the events of July 1952 as the 'overthrow' of the monarchy (*inqilab* in Arabic), where Nasser talked about a 'revolution' (*thawrah*).[65]

Others have suggested a conflict between generations – Naguib representing here an old-fashioned soldier, whose instincts told him that soldiers should be in their barracks, and politicians in parliament. Nasser by contrast was young, ambitious, and determined to use the army and the state to remake Egyptian society. Naguib himself suggested this explanation in his memoirs, saying Nasser believed 'with all the bravado of a man of 36, that we could afford to alienate every segment of Egyptian public opinion to achieve our goals. [66]

On 23 February Naguib announced his resignation as President. According to his own account, this was prompted by frustration that his power in the regime did not match his public role. He proposed that Nasser should learn the craft of ruling as his apprentice. 'I suggested that he allow me to run things for a few years until he acquired the experience necessary to succeed me, at which time, I assured him, I would gladly resign in his favour.' [67] Naguib's analysis of the crisis suggests that his main concern was consolidating his own power, rather than any genuine sympathy for parliamentary democracy, but his isolation in the Revolution Command Council prompted him to look outside the Free Officers' ranks for support.

Naguib's resignation followed months of tension at the heart of the regime. Behind Naguib's avuncular, plain-speaking façade, lay the mind of a shrewd politician. He used his position as Prime Minister and later as President to cultivate public support. On his regular tours of the country, he was met by cheering crowds. While the leadership of the Free Officers wrangled behind the scenes, he appeared to many ordinary people as the face of the army's revolution. For Khaled Mohi-al-Din, this was both Naguib's greatest strength and later his greatest weakness. In contrast to Nasser, Naguib appeared uninterested in the mechanics of government, preferring the 'appearances and aura of power'. 'Naguib, whether as president of the republic or as prime minister, never bothered to call me to ask about the two ministries I was supervising or about conditions in the cavalry. Nasser on the other hand was constantly in touch, always inquiring painstakingly about everything.'[68]

However, when it came to the final test of strength, it appeared at first as if Naguib, and not Nasser, had the upper hand. Naguib's resignation was accepted by the Revolution Command Council. Salah Salem explained to foreign journalists on 25 February that he wanted to establish a dictatorship. 'We had to break with Naguib who aimed at dictatorship, criticized in public and to foreigners decisions that had been made by a majority, and with no thought but his own popularity, played a double game by coming to an understanding with the opposition.'[69]

Few were convinced. For several months, Naguib had been dropping hints in press interviews that he opposed the continuing purge of the Free Officers' opponents. He was thought to be supported by Khaled Mohi-al-Din and the left-wing cavalry officers grouped around him. The news of his resignation was met with anger and disbelief in the streets. Khaled Mohi-al-Din came back from the cinema with his wife – where they had been to see *Julius Caesar* – to find an urgent summons to a meeting of the Revolution Command Council. He found the officers in a black mood. '"Peace be upon you all" I said. No one answered. They all sat there with cold, drawn faces. Nasser was holding his head in his hands ... Salah Salem said that his children at home had criticized him and that when his servant went shopping the shopkeepers in Abbassiya refused to sell him anything.[70]

Demonstrations began the following day. For once the opposition was united: cooperation between the officers' regime and the Brotherhood had broken down the previous month. Nasser ordered the dissolution of the Brotherhood in January 1954, after provoking a series of clashes with Brotherhood members at mosques across the country and in Cairo University. Now activists from the Brotherhood were joined on the streets by the Wafd and the left. The demonstrators demanded not only the reinstatement of Naguib, but also the lifting of censorship and the restoration of parliament. Opposition to the Revolution Command Council temporarily brought together an extremely diverse coalition: ranging from the landowners who hoped to bring a halt to the officers' revolution, to the Muslim Brotherhood, and to the Communists, by now united against Nasser.

However it was not the street protests which immediately preoccupied the Revolution Command Council, but the split in the army and the growing danger that a fratricidal conflict would tear the Free Officers apart. The chief opposition to the RCC's decision to accept Naguib's resignation came from the cavalry. Despite his isolation on the RCC, where his arguments in favour of restoring parliament and extending political free-doms found little support, Khaled Mohi-al-Din had built up his own network of left-leaning officers, who now called for Naguib's reinstatement.

The decisive encounter between the two factions in the army took place on 26 February. Naguib had been placed under house arrest. Cavalry officers met in the Green Mess Hall at their barracks to discuss the situation. At this tense moment Nasser arrived, hoping perhaps to pre-empt a dangerous split in the army ranks. He found the cavalry officers united against him, and in little mood to listen to listen to his argu-ments. The officers insisted Nasser's companions leave the room so that they could speak to him in private. The debate raged for hours into the night. At one point, Nasser heard the rumble of tanks outside the building. Ahmad al-Masri, Khaled Mohi-al-Din's brother, and one of the leaders of the cavalry officers, recalled later that Nasser paused, lit another cigarette and carried on speaking.[71]

Beneath his composure, Nasser was shaken. Tempers were

running high, he was alone and he had begun to fear that the cavalry officers were planning a coup. Khaled Mohi-al-Din later claimed that the movement of tanks outside the meeting was an attempt by some of the cavalry officers to improve their negotiating position by increasing psychological pressure on their opponent, but Nasser believed it was the first rumblings of a military strike against the RCC. He extricated himself from the meeting after accepting Naguib's return as President.

Initially the RCC agreed to Naguib's reinstatement, and Khaled Mohi-al-Din's appointment as Prime Minister. However, this was quickly overturned in favour of a new arrangement whereby Nasser would become Prime Minister. Demonstrations intensified after Naguib declared that his return was on the understanding that parliamentary life would also be restored. Huge crowds besieged the Abdin Palace in Cairo, where Naguib appeared on the balcony to acknowledge the cheers. Numerous activists from the Brotherhood were conspicuous in the crowd. At one point Abd-al-Qadir Awda, the Brotherhood's Deputy General Guide, appeared brandishing a handkerchief, which was stained with the blood of a young demonstrator who had been killed by the police in a nearby street.

On the 25 March, the Revolution Command Council lifted the ban on political parties, ended censorship and began to release political prisoners. In a terse communiqué the RCC announced 'the Council of the Revolution will surrender its powers to a constituent assembly on 24 July 1954 at which time it will proclaim the end of the Egyptian Revolution.'[72]

Burying Caesar

Nasser now moved into action. Using the apparatus of the Liberation Rally, the security services and his supporters in the unions, he orchestrated demonstrations and strikes to demand the continuation of the revolution. The turnout was patchy: in

Cairo a meeting of important union leaders voted to remain neutral while in Alexandria there was a general strike in favour of a return to democracy.[73] Officials from the Liberation Rally worked desperately to enforce the strike. They cut off the electricity to the Cairo trams and blocked the railway lines. Despite uneven support for the strikes and protests, within a few days the RCC had gone back on its decision to dissolve itself, postponed elections indefinitely, and re-introduced censorship. Mass arrests of opposition leaders and journalists quickly followed. Nasser also purged the army, arresting 16 cavalry officers who were later put on trial. Khaled Mohi-al-Din was sent into exile in Geneva.

Over the days that followed Nasser met dozens of delegations of workers. On 31 March he told representatives of the train drivers' and conductors' union: *There were 18 million people in this country with no party to represent them. They were deceived, helpless and misled ... anyone who raised his voice was forbidden even a morsel of bread, and they made war on his livelihood in order to enforce collective silence in the face of oppression, tyranny and exploitation. This is why our country was powerless until we made the revolution.* [74] On 2 April he met textile workers, and on 3 April public transport workers. On 6 April he told delegations of trade unionists from Alexandria and Suez: *Reaction will not triumph.*[75]

Yet the support Nasser could count on at this critical moment was real enough. A section of the middle class backed Nasser, fearing a return to the weak governments of the 1940s. Peasants who had benefited from the land reform feared the return of the feudal order – represented by some of the leaders of the political parties, such as Fu'ad Sirag al-Din of the Wafd. A section of the trade union movement was also prepared to support the RCC. Crucially, Nasser had the backing of key sections of the state – most of the army, the intelligence services, the media and the Liberation Rally. The Muslim Brotherhood also proved its worth to the regime; immediately on his release from jail, Hodeiby called on the nation to 'close ranks'. The Brotherhood's student members melted away from the protests on the campuses, deflating the pro-democracy movement. The rest of the opposition was furious, accusing the Brotherhood of having done a deal with the government.

It did not take Nasser long to conclude his victory. As his biographer Robert Stephens notes, Nasser's 'second coup, reminiscent in its timing and subtlety of Mark Antony's speech on the death of Caesar' was 'a masterful combination of force and political finesse.' [76]He had overcome the split in the army, and divided his civilian political opponents. On 17 April Naguib was forced to resign as Prime Minister in favour of Nasser. Although he remained president until October, he was now nothing more than a figurehead.

Clash with the Brotherhood

In the end, it was the Muslim Brotherhood which provided the opportunity to remove Naguib from power. Despite the appearance of coordination between the Brotherhood and Nasser over the end of the March crisis, relations between the two sides deteriorated rapidly over the summer of 1954. A crucial element in this change of tone was Nasser's deal with the British for the evacuation of the Canal Zone. Radical nationalists, including elements in the Brotherhood, accused Nasser of compromising with imperialism by concluding the agreement, which although it saw the departure of British troops from Egyptian soil, allowed for the reactivation of British bases in the event of an attack on pro-Western Turkey. Nasser himself knew that he had taken a risk in making concessions, but he felt the price was worth paying, as it would finally end more than 70 years of British military presence in Egypt. Anthony Nutting, who led Britain's negotiating team, described the scene at the ceremony to sign the agreement.

As he reached out to sign the document Nutting discovered his fountain pen had run out of ink, so he borrowed Nasser's. 'Having signed my name as an automatic reflex I put the pen in my breast-pocket. Nasser held out his hand and with a broad grin said, *I think you have already got enough out of me in this treaty. Please can I have my pen back?*'[77]

In Alexandria on 26 October the Brotherhood's verbal attacks on Nasser took a more lethal form. A member of the group's Secret Apparatus, Mahmud Abd-al-Latif, fired on Nasser as he was speaking to a public rally to celebrate Evacuation Day, marking the end of British occupation. The recording of the speech captures the moment when the would-be assassin struck. Nasser had paused in his speech when eight shots rang out from close to the stage. As panic swept the crowd, his voice was heard above the din. *Everyone stay where they are! Everyone stay where they are!* Mastering himself, his voice hoarse with emotion – a stark contrast to the smooth oratory of a few minutes before – he shouted his defiance: *My life is a sacrifice for you, oh men. Oh free people, my life is a sacrifice for you, my blood is a sacrifice for you. This is Gamal Abd-al-Nasser, speaking to you now . . . I am Gamal Abd-al-Nasser. I am of you and for you. My blood is for you . . . for your freedom and your dignity.*[78]

Within days Nasser had moved decisively to crush the Brotherhood. He told a rally in Cairo on his return: *the revolution shall not be crippled; if it is not able to proceed white, then we will make it red.*[79] Thousands of supporters of the Brotherhood were arrested, and a military tribunal condemned not only Mahmud Abd-al-Latif, but also the General Guide, his deputy and three other senior figures to death. All but Hodeiby were hanged. Naguib was formally deposed as President on the pretext that he had collaborated with the Brotherhood and the Communists.

His 'young man's bravado' had carried Nasser to the threshold of supreme political power, but it had made him feared rather

The trial of the Muslim Brothers accused of trying to assassinate Nasser

than loved. The news of the sentences on the Brotherhood's leaders brought a storm of protest around the Middle East. Few could have imagined that in less than two years this symbol of internal repression and external compromise would be transformed into the undisputed leader of the Arab world.

The high tide of liberation

It was not only in Egypt that the end of the Second World War heralded a revival of nationalism. From Iraq to Morocco, movements very similar to Egypt's took to the streets to demand the withdrawal of colonial troops. Across Africa, the Middle East and Asia, the old empires were crumbling. From Indo-China to Cairo, and from Malaya to Kenya, the old certainties of British and French rule were swept away.

In Syria, a nationalist uprising in 1946 forced the French to withdraw from the country, finally ending years of mandate rule. Iraq, nominally independent, but in reality still dominated by the British, was shaken by a series of strikes and student protests in 1948 and 1952. Algeria, scene of a long-running battle between the FLN nationalist movement and the French colonial authorities, exploded into civil war during 1954. After more than a decade of protest, the Moroccan nationalist movement forced France to concede independence in 1956.

The new movements had two main aims. The first goal was genuine independence, in place of tutelage under the paternalistic rule of European administrators or their local proxies. The second, which seemed impossible to achieve without the first, was a heady brew of progress, modernisation and economic growth harnessed for the good of the majority. A large part of the power of these movements lay in these demands for social justice. It was one reason why the idea of 'national liberation' inspired mass movements and not just coteries of intellectuals.

Standing in the way of these goals were the colonial powers, but also sometimes traditional rulers and landed 'feudal' elites. As the example of Egyptian agriculture shows, most of the 'feudalists' were nothing of the kind – they were fast becoming agro-capitalists of a very modern type – but the kind of social inequalities on which their wealth was based seemed to have more in common with the Middle Ages than the brave new world of the 20th century. Across the Middle East, society was changing rapidly. The national liberation movements were often led by members of new social classes – a growing urban middle class and in some cases urban workers - the disenfranchised and the dispossessed.

This created a dilemma for the leaders of the national liberation movements. If they supported workers against their employers, and peasants against their landlords, national unity would disintegrate. Yet it was often the landlords and factory owners who turned to the colonial powers to defend the existing social order against the demands of their fellow countrymen. Was the real enemy at home or abroad? As the civilian leaders of the national liberation movements struggled to answer this question, it was the army which took the initiative. Syria lived through a period of coups and counter-coups during the 1940s and 1950s; in Egypt the Free Officers took power while Iraq saw its own version of the 1952 revolution in 1958, when officers led by Abd-al-Karim Qassim overthrew the monarchy. In Egypt the army imposed social peace on an unruly movement and then turned to face the colonial powers. As Nasser put it in a speech in 1958 attacking the Communist Party: *we cannot fight Zionism and colonialism if we are divided.* [80]

In 1954, as Nasser emerged victorious from the struggles with Naguib and with the Muslim Brotherhood, his future role as a leader of the Arab world was not yet clear. In many Arab countries the Free Officers' regime was regarded with suspicion; the new government was seen as dangerously close to the USA. Three factors helped to push Nasser down the road towards his future role: the polarisation of international politics through the Cold War, attempts by the old colonial powers to claw back their fading influence in the region, and finally, continuing pressure on the Free Officers' regime to deliver economic and social development. One of Nasser's contemporary biographers sums up the attitude of many Egyptians in 1954: 'the average Egyptian seemed to accord him the reluctant and slightly awed respect that schoolboys give to a vigorous and high-minded headmaster who is determined to ginger up the standards of the school.'[81] By the end of the 1950s he had taken on a different character – the heir of Salah-al-Din and the champion of anti-colonial revolution.

The Philosophy of the Revolution

In these early days, the political underpinnings of Nasser's decisions were hardly robust. Unlike the ideological pan-Arabists of the Ba'ath Party in Syria and Iraq, Nasser and the Free Officers were at first propelled forward by the course of events rather than a grand vision of Arab unity. Nasser's short pamphlet, *The Philosophy of the Revolution*, which was written in 1953, provides a sketch of his ideas. In it he presented a picture of Egypt at the centre of three interlocking circles – the Arab, African and Islamic worlds.

The most important of these circles was the Arab world. In a highly personalised account of the Free Officers' role in the war of 1948, Nasser contrasted the Arabs' current weakness – and in particular the spinelessness of their traditional leaders – with their potential power. The first source of Arab power was their cultural and social heritage, which had given birth to three great monotheistic religions: Judaism, Christianity and Islam. Another card in Arab hands was the strategic position of the Middle East: *the world's meeting place; its commercial crossroads and military highway.*[82] The final source of power was the Arab world's oil wealth: *the nervous system of civilisation.*[83]

In Africa, the second circle in Nasser's scheme, Egyptians could not but see a reflection of their own struggle against colonialism. *We cannot, in any circumstances, whether we wanted to or not, stand aside from the bloody and terrifying struggle now taking place in the depths of Africa between five million whites and two hundred million Africans.* [84] Nasser then turned to the third circle, the Islamic world. Here he sketched another kind of unity, binding together the millions of Muslim believers across the world through shared rituals of faith. This potential power could be mobilised through political means, he suggested, by turning the pilgrimage to Mecca into a kind of international Islamic parliament, which would bring together the leading figures of the Muslim world.

Although Nasser included an Islamic circle in his vision of the future, his attitude to religion in politics was very different to that of his critics in the Muslim Brotherhood. He was devout as an individual, performing two pilgrimages to Mecca, one in 1954 and one in 1965. However he firmly resisted the demands of his critics in the Muslim Brotherhood for the Islamisation of the state. In later life he attempted to synthesize Islam and socialism, and promoted reform of Al-Azhar, the ancient Islamic university in Cairo.[85]

As he sat alone in his study, pondering these problems, his thoughts turned to Pirandello's play: *Six characters in search of an author.*[86] Nasser's choice of metaphor to describe the means to turn Arab, African and Muslim unity into reality was revealing. The stage was set, but the hero had not yet arrived.[87] *I look back to the wandering characters searching for someone to play them. This is the part. This is the text, and this is the stage. We alone are in place to take up the role.*[88]

The Philosophy of the Revolution was an early fruit of the relationship between Nasser and Muhammad Hassanein Heikal, later Egypt's best-known journalist and editor-in-chief of the semi-official daily *Al-Ahram*. Heikal encouraged Nasser to get his ideas into print, and according to some accounts, actually wrote the pamphlet himself.[89] Another story has it that Nasser's wife, Tahia, rescued the manuscript of *The Philosophy* from the wastepaper basket. Whatever the truth of that particular anecdote, with Heikal Nasser enjoyed both an immensely fruitful working relationship and a long-lasting personal friendship. 'Heikal approached Nasser as a friend, and not as a journalist eager for sensational stories. Both avid readers, Heikal and Nasser had a rare "meeting of minds" on various political and social matters.' [90]

During the 1940s the Egyptian press reflected the ideological battles of the day. Political allegiances dominated journalism, but the fragmentation of the establishment parties also created a space for opposition to emerge even in the mainstream press. Anwar Sadat spent several years as a journalist during this period, while Nasser himself also contributed articles to the magazine *Rose el-Youssef* under a pseudonym.[91] After the Free Officers took power, Nasser remained acutely concerned with the press. He read the first editions of the Egyptian papers every day, and read excerpts from the foreign press between midnight and going to bed each night.[92]

Nasser also had an eye for a good story. In 1955, he heard

Born in 1923, Muhammad Hassanein Heikal had already been working as a journalist for nearly ten years when he met Nasser in July 1952. Newly promoted to editor-in-chief of *Ahker Sa'a,* Heikal had come to interview Muhammad Naguib when Nasser and Amer arrived. Heikal suspected that something was afoot in the army. Five days later the officers took power.

Heikal later went on to edit *Al-Akhbar*, and became editor-in-chief at *Al-Ahram* in 1957, a post he held until 1974 when he was sacked by Nasser's successor, Anwar Sadat.

Still an influential voice in Egyptian politics, Heikal remains an uncompromising defender of Nasser's legacy.

about an English schoolboy, Howard Jones, who had run away from home. When asked why he had done so, Howard said that he desperately wanted to see the world, and in particular Egypt.

Nasser wrote to the schoolboy inviting him to visit – although this time with his mother. Howard and Mrs Jones took him up on the offer, and were given a tour of Egypt's tourist attractions, with a Pathé News cameraman in tow to capture it all for cinema audiences around the world.[93]

Nasser cultivated close relationships with a number of prominent journalists, including Heikal. By the late 1950s, Heikal had gained uniquely privileged access to Nasser. His columns were seen as authoritative statements of Nasser's views, and were read eagerly not only by Egypt's political elite, but also by diplomats and foreign politicians. Despite his increasingly important role, it was only in the last few years of Nasser's life that Heikal was given a post in government, as Minister for National Guidance.

Two visions of the Middle East

In 1952 Egypt's military revolution seemed precarious. The Free Officers' success was something of an anomaly. The independent, nationalist future Nasser was beginning to sketch out in his speeches, broadcast by Voice of the Arabs radio to the world, was a far cry from the reality of the Middle East. In Iraq, Jordan and much of the Gulf, conservative British-backed monarchs continued to rule. The Hashemite dynasty, in power in Iraq and Jordan, dreamed of uniting the Fertile Crescent under its crown. Syria, after all, had been the seat of King Faisal's first 'Arab kingdom' in 1918, before the French crushed the independence movement and imposed colonial control in 1920.

As consolation, the British had offered Faisal the throne of Iraq – despite strenuous protests by large numbers of Iraqis. By the 1950s, British control was more discreet, but the Prime Minister, Nuri al-Sa'id, could be relied upon to champion Western interests. He saw himself as a frontline fighter in the struggle against Communism, seeking link Iraq with pro-Western regimes in Turkey and Pakistan in the Baghdad Pact of 1955.

It was not only in the realm of foreign policy that Nuri and Nasser differed – although this would be clearer by the end of the 1950s than at the beginning. Iraq's economy was dominated by foreign capital and the landed elite. A powerful consortium of multinational companies controlled the country's oil industry. The railways were run by a British company, as was Iraq's biggest port in the southern city of Basra. Agriculture was controlled by a handful of wealthy landowners while millions of Iraqi peasants lived in poverty.

Faced with mounting pressure for both greater democracy and further economic develop-

One of the architects of the Hashemite monarchy in Iraq, Nuri al-Sa'id (1888-1958) was killed while trying to escape the crowds who besieged the Palace and the British embassy during the overthrow of the monarchy in 1958.

The son of a clerk, Nuri al-Sa'id switched sides from the Ottomans in 1916 to join the British-backed Arab revolt of Sharif Hussein of Mecca and his sons. The 'Sharifian' officers formed the core of the new state of Iraq, which was given to Faisal, Sharif Hussein's son as his kingdom by the British.

Many-times prime minister, Nuri al-Sa'id dominated Iraqi political life under the monarchy.

ment to ease the crushing poverty of Iraq's growing population, Nuri's main strategy was repression. Strikers were shot down, newspapers closed and Communist activists executed. Although he did implement a number of development projects – mainly financed by oil revenues – he could not afford to challenge the political power of the landowners. As early as 1946 even the British Embassy was wringing its hands in despair. A report from the chancery in Baghdad to the Foreign Office noted: 'with the old gang in power this country cannot hope to progress very far'.[94]

Despite this warning, Britain's long-term strategy for the Middle East depended on maintaining an alliance with the region's kings. The fall of the Egyptian monarchy and the Free Officers' assault on the political role of the landlords threatened to undermine the whole structure of colonial power. In 1956 Britain's violent response to that threat would later also provide a trigger for the confiscation of foreign companies and propel Nasser away from the free market towards national development through the state.

Cold War rivalry

In 1952 Nasser's conversion to state planning was still years in the future. In the early days following the coup, the Free Officers were thought by many on the left to have the support of the US government. Some US officials clearly thought that Nasser and his colleagues were sympathetic to their aims. Miles Copeland later described how he and his colleagues in the CIA decided that what Egypt needed was a 'Muslim Billy Graham', and that they thought they had found him in Nasser.[95] State Department advisers helped the new government draw up the plans for land reform. At first the US had little to fear from the new regime's economic policies. Hoping to attract overseas investment, the Free Officers reintroduced majority foreign ownership of Egyptian firms and tamed the trade unions through repression.

Yet rather than find a new imperial patron to replace Britain, Nasser attempted to steer Egypt along a narrow path – refusing to chose one side or the other but open to offers of help from both Cold War camps. Global conflict projected his voice onto the world stage – at the Bandung Conference of 1955 he appeared next to established leaders, such as Tito of Yugoslavia, and Nehru of India, as an apostle of the new doctrine of 'Non-Alignment'. The world's poorest countries would be the losers if they allowed themselves to be sucked into the superpowers' arms race, Nasser told the conference. *There is a close connection between raising the standard of living of the people and decreasing the armaments burden. It is also evident that modern science and technology, if utilised for peaceful purposes, offer the possibility of greater well-being for the human race, than has ever been known.*[96]

In the meantime, Egypt's lack of arms and funding for the proposed High Dam at Aswan preyed on Nasser's mind and in both areas he favoured an agreement with the Western powers. By 1955 both were becoming urgent concerns. Development funding was crucial to maintaining Nasser's domestic power base; without further economic growth, the impact of the land reforms would soon recede. He had only to look at the fate of Syria's army regime, overthrown in February 1954 by a popular uprising under the watchword 'no more dictatorships'[97], to see one possible version of his own future. A radical foreign policy could also serve as a powerful unifier in a country still smarting from the forced departure of Muhammad Naguib and the crushing of the Muslim Brotherhood.

In the bi-polar world of the Cold War, both superpowers often looked with suspicion on attempts by other nations to chart a path between East and West. Yet for many Third World leaders of Nasser's generation, non-alignment or positive neutralism allowed them to benefit from both US and Soviet aid, without placing their countries in either camp. Thus until the 1960s, despite Nasser's fierce anti-imperialist rhetoric, Egypt's loans and aid came from the USA and USSR in roughly equal measures.

The Bandung Conference in 1955 was followed by the Non-Aligned Summit Conference in Belgrade in 1961, which set up the Non-Aligned Movement.

The need to re-equip Egypt's army was underlined by a large-scale Israeli raid on the Gaza Strip in February 1955. Thirty-nine Egyptians and Palestinians died on what had been a quiet frontier. Despite the young officers' burning shame at the humiliation of defeat in 1948, Nasser had shown no desire for military confrontation with Israel. Consolidating power at home and securing British withdrawal were far more important to the Free Officers' regime. The Gaza raid changed all that. He now came under severe pressure to give the Egyptian army and the Palestinian refugees crowded into the Gaza Strip the means to defend themselves.

General Burns, Chief of Staff of the UN forces, explained Nasser's dilemma. 'Shortly before the raid, he had visited Gaza and told the troops that there was no danger of war; that the Gaza Armistice Demarcation Line was not going to be a battle-front. After that many of them had been shot in their beds. Never again could he risk telling the troops they had no attack to fear; never again could he let them believe they could relax their vigilance.'[98]

Nasser's approaches to the US for arms were rebuffed, however, and by September 1955 he had negotiated an arms deal with Czechslovakia, gaining Egypt access to the Soviet arsenal. Despite this, both the British Ambassador to Egypt, Humphrey Trevelyan, and his American counterpart, argued with their governments to stop Nasser going to Moscow for funding for the High Dam by sealing a deal for western aid. But British and American policy was changing. Nuri al-Sa'id of Iraq complained bitterly that Egypt's independent line seemed to produce more aid than his own policy of cooperation. Not for the first time, Nuri's annoyance seemed to find an echo in Washington, where Secretary of State Dulles wanted to turn aid flows from 'neutralists', such as Nasser, who manoeuvred between the rival Cold War camps, to allies of the US. The desire to deliver a blow to the USSR also came into play – Dulles believed that he could call the Russians' bluff by withdrawing the American offer to support Egypt's application for a loan from the World Bank to build the dam, and thus forcing them to 'choose between backing down or investing in a project they could not afford.'[99]

As early as 1953, US State Department's Office of Near Eastern Affairs had argued strongly against economic assistance for Egypt. A confidential memo written in December that year set out the dangers posed to US interests by the Free Officers' support for 'neutralism'. 'In Iraq and Jordan many a politician and army officer will wonder if the best way to get US support is not to abrogate their treaties with Britain (and the IPC [Iraq Petroleum Company] concession) and engage in an all-out campaign against 'imperialism'. The idea will spread that the surest way to open Uncle Sam's pocket-book (and maybe his arsenals) is to move towards neutralism or 'pro-Communism' and point out that your country is bound to fall to the Russians unless the US steps in.'[100]

Algeria

As the drama of the Czech arms deal and the negotiations over the loan for the High Dam unfolded, Nasser's support for the cause of national liberation in North Africa was setting the scene for a confrontation with France. For Algerian rebels like Ahmed Ben Bella, the Free Officers' revolution transformed Egypt from an insecure temporary refuge into an ally in the struggle for liberation. In 1954, Ben Bella, who had arrived in Cairo two years earlier, was one of the nine founding members of the Revolutionary Committee of Unity and Action (Comité Révolutionnaire d'Unité et d'Action - CRUA) of the Algerian National Liberation Front (Front de Libération National - FLN). For a while the headquarters of the North African liberation movements on Abd-al-Khaleq Tharwat Street was a hub of the anti-colonial revolution.

With Ben Bella in Algeria

The fight against colonialism in Algeria was more bitter and bloody than in Egypt. With a large population of French settlers in Algeria, the French authorities could not afford to cut their losses and pull out as the British were doing in Egypt. After the FLN launched a nation-wide insurrection against French rule in Algeria on 1 November 1954, troops poured across the Mediterranean. By 1956 there were 400,000 French soldiers in Algeria, and sporadic guerrilla raids had become all-out war.

From Nasser the Algerian insurgents received more than words of solidarity, Ben Bella later recalled: 'the first Suez Canal proceeds after nationalisation were presented to us, the FLN leaders, by Gamal Abd-al-Nasser. How can I not be a Nasserist?' [101] Broadcasts from Cairo relayed the message of the exiled FLN leaders back to Algeria. The French government was convinced that Egypt was supplying arms to the FLN. On 16 October 1956, the Sudanese-flagged ship *Athos* was seized by the French navy en route to deliver arms to the FLN through Morocco. Six days later a plane carrying Ben Bella, Ait Ahmed and other FLN leaders from Morocco to an FLN conference in Tunisia was forced to land in Algiers by the French Air Force. Ben Bella would spend the next nine years in prison, before emerging triumphant to become Algeria's first Prime Minister in 1962.

The countdown to Suez

So despite the Cold War back-drop, Britain and France took centre stage at Suez in 1956. Britain hoped to reassert her influence over a country which had only just negotiated the withdrawal of British troops, and France was itching to punish Nasser for his support of the Algerian nationalists. And it was the old powers who over-reached themselves, inviting Israel to join the attack on Egypt but suffering political humiliation on the field of their military victory.

In May 1956 Nasser met Humphrey Trevelyan, the British Ambassador in Cairo. Trevelyan suggested a period of quiet on both sides, after the successful conclusion of British withdrawal. Nasser replied that Egypt could not remain indifferent to what was happening in the surrounding area. Trevelyan concluded that Nasser regarded himself as 'the destined champion of Arab nationalism' and was 'at heart still a revolutionary conspirator'.' Nasser told the ambassador: *You cannot carry out a gun-boat policy against me as you could against Farouq. I have no throne, no hereditary position, no fortune.* [102]

Just two months later, warned by the Egyptian Ambassador to Washington that the US might withdraw its offer of support for the High Dam project, Nasser accepted the proposals unconditionally. A few days later, however, Dulles abruptly withdrew the offer in a manner which seemed designed to humiliate Nasser and underscore the US administration's hostility to 'neutralism'. Within days, Nasser had set in motion plans to nationalize the Suez Canal. In a speech on 24 July 1956 he attacked the US decision, addressing the US government directly: *I turn to them and say: 'You may die of your fury, for you will not rule us or tyrannise us. We know our way – the road of freedom, honour, dignity and glory.'* [103]

Two days later, tens of thousands gathered in Manshiyya Square in Alexandria – the very spot where Nasser had survived assassination only two years before – to hear him speak on the fourth anniversary of the overthrow of King Farouq. Nasser had been elected President just a month before in a referendum which followed the adoption of a new constitution in January 1956. Journalists accustomed to Nasser's usual formal – some might say austere and even awkward – style of speaking were taken by surprise as he joked with the crowd in colloquial Egyptian, the *baladi* tongue of the street. French journalists Jean and Simone Lacouture describe the scene.

'Now I'll fill you in on my adventures with the American diplomats . . . The orator put on a comic act in mime, playing the part of the Egyptian comic, Goha, struggling against the foreign Goliaths ... the shy and awkward Nasser had suddenly discovered how to talk to the Egyptian people. Down below us, in the dark bowl of the Muhammad Ali Place, there was no longer seething anger but an enormous laughter that had to be heard to be believed.'[104] Nasser turned his anger on Eugene Black, President of the World Bank, who reminded him of Ferdinand de Lesseps, owner of the Suez Canal company, and, Nasser said, a proponent of *mortgage colonialism.*

'*Everything which was stolen from us by that imperialist company, that state within a state, when we were dying of hunger, we are going to take back ... The government has decided on the following law: a presidential decree nationalising the International Suez Canal Company. In the name of the nation, the president of republic declares the International Suez Canal Company an Egyptian limited company.* There was uproar all around us. Journalists we knew to be sceptical of the government were standing on their chairs, shouting enthusiastically, while Nasser – suddenly seized with a fit of laughing at his own cheek – continued: *Now, as I am speaking to you, your brothers, sons of Egypt are directing the Canal Company and carrying out the work of the company. Now, right this minute, they are taking over the Canal Company, the Egyptian Canal Company not the foreign Canal Company . . . the Canal which is on Egyptian soil, the Canal which is part of Egypt, now belongs to Egypt.*[105]

The operation ran like clockwork: a pre-arranged code-word – the hissing syllables 'de Lesseps' – gave Egyptian forces their marching orders. As the soldiers overran the company headquarters, the managing director of the Suez Company was having dinner with the governor of Ismailiyya, listening to Nasser's speech broadcast live on the radio.

In London and Paris, the reaction was severe. British Prime Minister Anthony Eden and his Foreign Secretary John Selwyn-Lloyd denounced Nasser. French Prime Minister Guy Mollet described Nasser's pamphlet, *The Philosophy of the Revolution,* as a new version of Hitler's *Mein Kampf.* Nasser's chief opponent in the Arab world, Iraqi Prime Minister Nuri al-Sa'id, was also apparently keen to see the Egyptian leader humbled. He was with King

Raising the Egyptian flag

Faisal at a state dinner held at 10 Downing Street when the news of Nasser's announcement arrived. His advice to Eden about Nasser was swift: 'Hit him hard, and hit him now'.[106]

Widely seen as a natural heir to Britain's war-time leader, Winston Churchill, Anthony Eden (1897-1977) took office in 1955 having served as Foreign Secretary in Churchill's cabinet.

In 1956, his response to Nasser's nationalisation of the Suez Canal split Britain. Eden argued later 'I thought and think that failure to act would have brought the worst of consequences just as I think the world would have suffered less if Hitler had been resisted on the Rhine'. However, his decision to involve British troops in retaking the Canal brought condemnation from Britain's major ally, the United States, and sparked protests at home.

He fell ill during the Suez Crisis, and resigned as Prime Minister in January 1957.

Egyptians, however, greeted the news with joy, as the Lacoutures found on their return to Cairo. 'We felt the full force of the people's frenzy in Cairo two days later, when the *Bikbashi* (Lieutenant Colonel) came back, suddenly promoted to the status of national hero. You had to have seen the erst-while timid staff-officer, the morose Gamal Nasser of yester-day, the timid technocrat, to see the change in him now as he was lifted above the heads of a howl-ing mob, waving his arms like a drowning man on the boiling sea – a boxing champion return-ing in triumph to his native Chicago … There was the same approval in the poorer cafés and in society drawing-rooms – "He did the right thing, he has made a fool of the people who wanted to get rid of him, the whole country's been waiting for something like this for a long time and we'll have to see it through."'[107]

Whatever foreign journalists felt about the fickle emotions of 'the mob', Nasser's decision connected with deep currents in Egypt's political soul. Thousands of Egyptians died to build the Canal in the 1860s and the debts incurred by the Khedives in order to finance it brought the country under foreign occupation in 1882. More than half a century later, thousands of Egyptian volunteers fought a guerrilla war against the British in the Canal Zone, forcing a withdrawal in 1954. After all this, here was Nasser laughing in the face of the world powers, reminding them that Egypt too, was a nation, Egypt too, had her pride.

In practical terms, the nationalisation decree was less momentous than the bluster from London and Paris suggested. Nasser offered compensation for the foreign shareholders, and agreed to abide by international treaties guaranteeing right of passage through the canal. The 99-year concession under which the company operated had reached its final decade, and on its expiry complete control of the canal would revert to Egypt. The company itself was an Egyptian enterprise, albeit one with foreign governments as shareholders.

Since the Second World War, the only country whose flag had not been allowed to pass the Canal was Israel, as Egypt considered the banning of passage of Israeli ships 'indispensable to the defence of the country'. Egyptian lawyers cited the Constantinople Convention of 1888 to justify their government's action – the treaty gave Egypt the right to restrict the passage of ships 'should it prove necessary to her defence or the maintenance of public order'.[108]

A hard-headed look at the financial balance sheet might have called Nasser's judgment into question. The Canal was unlikely to produce the kind of revenue which Egypt needed to construct the High Dam quickly enough. However, as both Nasser and his opponents in the West understood, the nationalisation of the Canal Company was above all a supreme act of political defiance. Its meaning was clear: to Egypt's former imperial masters it was a gesture of independence, while to the USA, which was well on the way to replacing Britain and France as the dominant power in the Middle East, it was a warning – Egypt had not expended so much blood in ridding herself of one type of colonialism to be ensnared a second time.

On one level, Nasser clearly miscalculated. He believed that Britain and France, the two powers most directly affected by the seizure of the Canal, would be unlikely to take military action against Egypt, as both were preoccupied with protecting their other interests in the Middle East – Britain in Iraq and Iran, and France in North Africa, where French troops were engaged in a bitter war with the nationalist movement. Nasser guessed, correctly as it turned out, that the US would not favour a military solution to the issue. He also did not consider it likely that either France or Britain would find an ally in Israel.

As tension mounted through the summer months, in public Nasser remained defiant. At a press conference on 12 August he spoke to the foreign media. *I realise that the British newspapers, almost all the British newspapers, are telling the British public that Egypt nationalised the company. Nasser seized the company, Nasser grabbed the company . . . Well it is not true. It is a misinterpretation. The canal is an Egyptian canal. It is part of our territory.* Freedom of navigation would be guaranteed, Nasser promised, but there could be no compromising Egypt's sovereignty. He made clear that proposals to set up an international body to oversee the Canal smacked of colonialism. *We got rid of colonialism, British occupation, we are not going to accept by any means another sort of colonialism, another sort of collective colonialism, however it is disguised.* [109]

In private, however, he was beginning to consider the possibility of military defeat. He asked Muhammad Hassanein Heikal to prepare secret plans for a guerrilla war of national liberation, should the colonial powers succeed in re-occupying Egypt.

The attack

In the event, only one of Nasser's assumptions turned out as predicted: the US did not support military action. Britain, France and Israel, however, jointly planned and executed a ferocious assault – which has gone down in Egyptian history as 'the

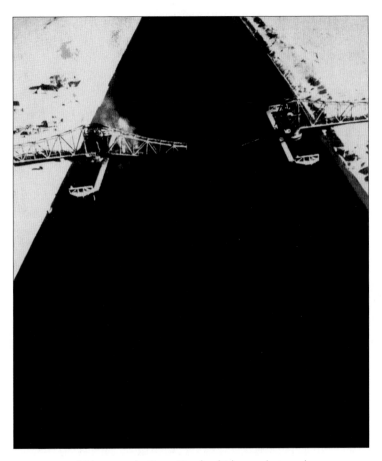

Bridge over the Suez Canal, which was destroyed
during the fighting in 1956

Tripartite Aggression' – leaving Britain and France in control of
the Canal Zone, and Israel occupying the Sinai Peninsula.

On 29 October, Israeli troops crossed the border into Egypt
near the small border post of Kuntilla. Taking advantage of the
darkness they surprised and overwhelmed Egyptian forces in the
area before moving on to capture most of the Sinai Peninsula. The
general in charge of the offensive was Moshe Dayan. Despite some

moments when stiff Egyptian resistance slowed the Israeli advance, there was little Nasser could do but pull his troops back to defend the Canal.

A joint ultimatum by the British and French governments was announced that afternoon. Both Egyptian and Israeli forces were to withdraw to a distance of ten miles on each side of the Canal, to allow French and British troops to occupy the Canal Zone in order to protect 'freedom of navigation'.[110] The Israelis were happy to accept – they had not even reached the Canal by the time the ultimatum had been announced – but for the Egyptians it meant a further retreat before the Israeli advance, and the undoing of all that had been won so painfully during the struggle to end British occupation. Nasser rejected the ultimatum, and on 31 October British and French planes launched a wave of attacks on Cairo and the Canal Zone cities.

An early member of the Free Officers and member of the Command Council, Salah Salem, supported Nasser in 1954, despite differences over Egyptian policy towards his birthplace, Sudan.

The following year, he was sent to negotiate with Nuri al-Sa'id over Iraq's proposals to create a pro-western alliance with Turkey and Pakistan. Nuri emerged from the talks claiming that Salah Salem had given his approval for the Baghdad Pact, despite Salem's denials and Nasser's unremitting hostility to the idea. He resigned as Minister of National Guidance in September 1955, and became editor of *Al-Sha'ab* newspaper.

Nasser was at home receiving the Indonesian Ambassador when he heard the first bombs hit Cairo airport. After rushing up to the roof to see British and French bombers flying overhead, he made for the Commander-in-Chief's office, 'where he found a confusion of men and ideas, everyone talking at the same time.' According to Muhammad Hassanein Heikal's account, his old comrades were in a blind panic: Salah Salem suggested that Nasser should give himself up to the American embassy and sue for peace.[111]

Small girl in the wreckage of Port Said during
the Anglo-French invasion of 1956

When British and French bombs put Cairo's radio station out of action,
Nasser went to the Al-Azhar mosque to rally the people.

In a speech ten years later Nasser recalled how he drove through the streets of Cairo that night, listening to the crowds who called out to him 'We shall fight, we shall fight'.[112] When British and French bombs put Cairo's radio station out of action, he went to the Al-Azhar mosque to rally the people. *For everyone of us, among the armed forces and the people, our watchword will be: 'we will fight and we will not surrender'. ... I am in Cairo and I will fight with you against any invasion. ... We will defend our country, our history and our future.*[113] The recording of the speech ended with an impassioned pledge to Nasser's listeners. Switching to pure Cairene dialect Nasser departed from his prepared text to speak directly to ordinary Egyptians, telling them that his own family shared their peril. *My children are here with you in Cairo . . . I haven't sent them away. I won't send them away while I'm here with you in Cairo . . . we will fight, as I told you yesterday, to the last drop of blood.*[114]

Faced with the combined force of two Great Powers, in addition to Israel's experienced troops, Nasser knew that Egypt's army could not hold out long. Training by Russian instructors had yet to make a real impact on the armed forces, and in any case, once Britain and France brought to bear their full military weight, the Egyptians would be hopelessly out-gunned. However, neither the Israelis, who had scored a decisive victory in the desert largely because they were mobile and had the advantage of surprise, nor the British and French, were prepared to fight their way house by house through Cairo. The British knew all too well the difficulties of maintaining a military occupation in a hostile country – they had withdrawn from the Canal Zone only two years before because the occupation could serve no useful purpose in the face of mass, armed opposition. And ordinary Egyptians, far from rushing to overthrow 'the apprentice dictator' of Eden's speeches, mobilized themselves to defend their homes and their country.

Nasser authorized the issue of 400,000 rifles to civilians and announced the formation of a people's militia. Hundreds of popular resistance groups sprang up across the country. In many cases it was Nasser's opponents who led the way, including Muslim Brotherhood, Communist and trade union activists who had suffered from the repression of the left in the period since the revolution. Even foreign journalists noticed the change in the public mood. Jean-Jacques Faust of Agence France Presse saw at first hand the militia, hastily re-titled the 'Liberation Army', lead stiff resistance in Port Said.

'From the time when the government called on them to defend their country and enrolled and armed them, inviting them to unite in their hatred of the foreigner (and almost inevitably 'the rich') a radical change came over those 'God-forgotten men' whom nobody had seemed to need before and who had always seemed to toil from day to day. Only some change of consciousness, of self-awareness, can explain the seriousness and sense of self-imposed discipline of the Liberation Army volunteers ... As a result it is impossible for the regime to go back to what it was before the Suez affair. In this sense, the Suez expedition has weakened Nasser's position as much as strengthened it. It has obliged the dictator to run the risk of a "real revolution"'.[115]

The real army did not fare so well, however. Abd-al-Hakim Amer, facing his first real test as Commander-in-Chief, refused to withdraw from Sinai. Nasser had phoned the operations room himself to make sure the order was carried out. Under the pressure of events, the army chain of command seemed to be disintegrating. The contrast between the regular army and the popular militias was most marked in Port Said. There, after hours of heavy fighting, the commander of the garrison began surrender talks. Nasser ordered the civilian governor to resist at all costs, and within two hours, militia units were taking to the streets to defend the city. The battle cost between 650 and 1000 Egyptian

Formation of a people's militia

dead, as the untrained and lightly armed civilians fought with British paratroopers. However, it served as a warning to the invaders that Egyptians would resist a new occupation.

Egypt was also not without support in the Arab world. Syrian army engineers put the Iraq Petroleum Company pumping stations out of action, while Saudi Arabia banned oil exports to Britain and France. Nasser, meanwhile, ordered the Canal blocked – 48 ships were quickly sunk in the waterway.

Meanwhile international pressure on Britain and France was mounting by the hour. On 2 November, the United Nations General Assembly passed a resolution calling for an immediate ceasefire and the withdrawal of Israeli forces to the armistice lines of 1948. Events were quickly moving out of the control of Anthony Eden and French Prime Minister Guy Mollet. As Egyptian forces fell back towards the Canal, there was a real danger that Israeli troops might complete the work of occupying Sinai before British and French forces could invade, thus removing the need for them to 'separate the warring sides'. There was also the threat that the USSR and USA might force a settlement, as diplomats sat in session late into the night at the UN. Despite being preoccupied with events in Hungary – Russian tanks rolled into Budapest on 4 November – the USSR intervened decisively in Nasser's favour. On 6 November, as British paratroopers landed in Port Said and French paratroopers in Port Fu'ad, Soviet Premier Bulganin threatened Britain, France and Israel with nuclear rocket attack.

Although the United States was quick to warn that any attack on Britain and France by Russia would bring American retaliation, US officials also put pressure on Eden and Mollet to withdraw. Dulles made it clear that US support to offset the cost of finding alternative oil supplies would only be forthcoming if Anglo-French forces got out as quickly as they had come. Around two weeks after the invasion Britain and France had agreed to leave and by the end of December their troops had withdrawn from Suez. Eden resigned as Prime Minister in January 1957.

So in the end Nasser's gamble paid off. Britain, France and Israel were forced to withdraw. On the Arab stage, he appeared for the first time as an expression of Arab pride, a leader who had humbled the old imperial powers and maintained his independence of the superpowers.

Al-Ra'is: the making of a myth

Nasser's transformation into a hero of Arab nationalism also marked a change in his personal relations with the remaining leaders of the Free Officers. During its first few years in power, the Command Council had retained some of the camaraderie of the barracks. Decision-making was still in theory collective, although in practice Nasser usually got his way if he wanted. By 1956 things had changed. Khaled Mohi-al-Din, returning to Egypt after a spell of exile in Geneva, was surprised to find Nasser's old comrades addressing him formally as 'Al-Ra'is' – president or chief – where before they had been on first-name terms. They stood up when he entered and left the room.[116]

Foreign journalists were also beginning to pay more attention to Egypt's leader. Western reporters were fascinated by his dark good looks and commanding physique. His tall figure reminded Jean Lacouture of 'a statue from the Cairo museum, in heavy, high-relief granite.'[117] Nasser's lifestyle also made a strong impression on contemporary observers. 'His personal habits are exemplary. He lives with complete lack of ostentation in a modest Cairo villa, and his personal life has been happy. He has five youthful children. He is a devout Muslim and does not touch alcohol,' wrote John Badeau, former President of the American University in Cairo, in 1959.[118] Nasser's image was not simply a public relations exercise; beyond providing a comfortable middle-class lifestyle for his wife and children he appears to have been largely uninterested in the personal trappings of power. What concerned him more was its substance.

Nasser's Jacobin incorruptibility was also said to have infuriated some of his enemies. The CIA's agents in Cairo in the fifties complained bitterly that he had none of the usual peccadilloes. 'The problem with Nasser is that he has no vices. We can neither buy nor blackmail him. We hate this guy's guts, but we can't touch him: he's too clean.'[119]

Founded in July 1953, Voice of the Arabs, *Sawt Al-Arab* in Arabic, broadcast Nasser's challenge to imperialism to a regional audience. As Nasser's influence rose, Voice of the Arabs' blend of polemic, passionate invective and nationalist songs attracted new listeners. For some this was the golden age of Arab radio. Others see the station's legacy differently, arguing that Voice of the Arabs offered little more than crude propaganda, and hampered the development of independent journalism in region.

Voice of the Arabs' credibility was severely compromised after the Six Day War in 1967, when Arab listeners learnt of Israel's gains from the Western media.

There was another side to Nasser's public persona: his distance from his old comrades was part of his projection of what Ghali Shoukri calls 'his metaphysical faith in his own union with the people.'[120] In his rhetoric of the period, Nasser spoke directly to 'the people' in his own name, the collective decision-making of the early days had long vanished. 'His decision is democracy itself, his thought is the people, and technical means are the modern substitute for the party in an under-developed country.'[121]

Nasser's skills as an orator played a crucial role in the creation of 'Al-Ra'is'. Perhaps his most enduring legacy has been the impact of his rhetoric on the Arabic language itself. He spoke at hundreds of meetings, many times covering several rallies on the same day. Many other Arab leaders, particularly those who, formally at least, held the same nationalist or socialist ideals as he did, followed his example in bringing the everyday language of the street into the realm of high politics.

The registers of modern Arabic are more varied, and lie further apart than modern English. Arab children grow up speaking a dialect of Arabic, but this colloquial language is almost never written down. At school they will be taught standard Arabic, which is the language of literature and the media. If they are Muslims, they will probably also be taught to read and understand classical Arabic, the language of the Qur'an – essentially the dialect of 7th-century Arabia. In a society where only the privileged few had access to education at all, Nasser's audiences were remarkably sensitive to language register as a marker for social status and authority.

Under the monarchy, most politicians used ornate, high-flown rhetoric. Nasser's approach was different. Rather than abandon standard Arabic altogether – and thus lose his ability to address audiences outside Egypt who spoke other Arabic dialects – Nasser adopted a technique of switching registers. In a speech in 1965 discussing the definition of socialism he introduces an imaginary questioner, who pipes up in Cairene dialect to demand a simpler explanation. Nasser starts off saying that socialism can be defined as: *The correct . . . interpretation of the revolution in terms of progressive action.* The speech then becomes a dialogue as Nasser takes the part of the audience: *But what's 'socialism' mean, then?* He answers his own question in the same formal language that he used initially, but the meaning is clearer and the sentence structure simpler: *'Socialism', in a word means the establishment of a society of sufficiency and justice . . . the establishment of a society of equal opportunity.*[122]

By the 1960s, Nasser had broadcast hundreds of hours of speeches using this technique, but during the mid-1950s, when he first adopted it, his style was a dramatic signal that in the officers' new republic, politics was no longer the preserve of the elite. It was also through his speeches, far more than his published writings, that he developed his ideas. His speeches are peppered with key phrases – dignity, freedom, glory, unity – which he repeated time and time again. These concepts were rarely explained. Instead, his most powerful speeches were those which marked a step putting theory into practice – such as the nationalisation of the Suez Canal. In this context, the meaning of dignity and freedom was clear: denying others the right to control Egypt's political and economic destiny.

His public performances also marked his transformation from conspirator to nationalist icon. Nasser's first major speech at Shibin al-Kum in February 1953, marking the launch of the Liberation Rally, was a stage-managed affair. The Lieutenant Colonel comes across as an effective speaker, but his self-conscious pauses to allow the Rally's officials to lead chanting in the crowd give the proceedings an air of unreality. In his later speeches the awkwardness has gone. There is no longer a need to whip up emotion from the crowd, in fact he often has to call for quiet to allow him to continue his speech above the cheers.

Family life

Another image began to emerge during the late 1950s complementing the larger-than-life figure of Al-Ra'is: Nasser as a devoted father and husband. Unlike her more glamorous successors, Jehan Sadat and Suzanne Mubarak, Tahia never played an independent political role as Egypt's 'First Lady'. After Nasser's rise to power, she brought up the couple's children in the small oasis of middle-class domestic bliss they created in the villa in Manshiet al-Bakry. Pictures of Tahia on the beach, or in the garden with the children, are a far cry from the images of power-dressing Arab leaders' wives today. United by a deep affection rather than shared ambition, their marriage appears to have been happy and fulfilling.

Tahia's role as mother and housewife did not mean that she was excluded from public life. Far from it: Nasser's habit of receiving official guests at home, rather than in the opulent splendour of one of the old royal palaces, created a continuous procession of world leaders through her living room. She accompanied him to public functions and sometimes on foreign visits. The children also met their share of VIPs. A photograph taken in 1964 shows Nasser, every inch the proud, beaming father, introducing his youngest son Abd-al-Hakim to the boxer Muhammad Ali.

The President, relaxing *en famille*: playing chess

Filming his
wife during
a holiday on
the beach

Introducing his son Abd-al-Hakim to the boxer Muhammad Ali, 1964

Despite this, and again unlike the more recent crop of Arab leaders, Nasser and Tahia clearly had no plans to found a political dynasty. Their two daughters, Hoda and Mona, and three sons, Khaled, Abd-al-Hamid and Abd-al-Hakim, were able to grow up sheltered from the tumultuous events of the 1950s, despite their famous father. Hoda describes living as simply an 'ordinary Egyptian girl of my generation'.[123] Hoda and Khaled did later take up political careers – Hoda now runs a research centre dedicated to preserving Nasser's legacy and Khaled became an MP – but they did not receive the kind of helping hand into the higher echelons of the state machine given to the sons of Syrian strongman Hafiz al-Asad, or Egyptian President Hosni Mubarak.

Nasser, Tahia and the family

Nor is there any evidence that this is what Nasser would have wanted. He hated hereditary privilege and went out of his way to ensure that his children were not given special favours, reminding them of his origins in the village of Beni Murr: *I am all the more proud to be a member of a poor family from that village, and I say these words as history is my witness that Nasser was born of a poor family and I promise that he will live and die a poor man.* His most recent biographer, Said Aburish, relates that when Nasser wanted to buy Mona and Hoda apartments of their own, his colleagues had to secretly make a collection for him to bridge the gap between his modest savings and the real cost of the flats.[124]

The United Arab Republic

1958 was the 'year of victory', 'the sunlit summit' of Egypt's power and influence. It was in this year that the balance of power in the Middle East seemed to shift decisively towards the rising tide of Arab nationalism. On 1 February 1958, Nasser stood with President Shukri al-Quwatli of Syria in Damascus and announced the formation of a new state, the United Arab Republic. Nasser told the huge crowd which had gathered to witness the event: *Today, the slogans of Arab nationalism became a reality. Today!*[125]

The formation of the UAR, and the dissolution of Egypt and Syria within it, had its roots in the internal dynamics of the national liberation movements. The radicalisation of Syrian politics, and in particular the rise of the Communists and the growing interest of the USSR in Syria, were one factor pushing the union to conclusion. [126] Sections of the army looked to Nasser to bring the Syrian Communists to heel, as he had already done in Egypt.

Nasser's championship of the Arab cause, and in particular the nationalisation of the Suez Company, had transformed him from a figure of hate in Syria to a national hero between 1954 and 1958. Huge demonstrations in support of him during the

Demonstrations in support of unity between Egypt and Syria: the novelist Naguib Mahfouz is in the picture with a group of intellectuals.

Suez Crisis demonstrated the popularity of his policies, and the Syrian army offered to invade Israel after the attack on Sinai. The Syrian government also gave its backing to Nasser; Shukri al-Quwatli, the President, flew to Moscow at the height of the crisis to urge Soviet support for Egypt.

Despite this façade of unity between the army, the politicians and the people, in reality Syria was deeply divided. Like Egypt, the 1940s and 1950s in Syria were a period of political turmoil, with many of the same forces locked in struggle. Unlike Egypt, Syria had achieved independence and the withdrawal of foreign forces relatively quickly. After a brief struggle in 1946, French forces abandoned their mandate. The government which replaced the old mandate authorities was initially dominated by the traditional leaders of the nationalist movement – large landowners and the urban notables of the merchant class.

The inability of the new government to deal with pressing social issues set the scene for the rise of more radical movements. The Syrian Communist Party was led by Khalid Bakdash, the first Communist to win a seat in parliament in the Arab world. The Arab Ba'ath Socialist Party, founded by Michel Aflaq and Salah-al-Din al-Bitar, linked a movement of poor peasants to the discontented urban middle class. The Ba'ath party's support of Arab unity seemed to dovetail with Nasser's thinking, although the party itself was a civilian and not a military movement, and later became Nasser's bitter enemy. In 1957, however, the Ba'ath party was one of the main forces in Syria pushing for closer ties to Egypt. Motivated in part by the realisation that their rivals in the Communist Party were gaining ground, Ba'ath leaders looked to closer links with Egypt as a bulwark against the left, and as a means to overcome the fragmentation of Syrian political life.

The Arab Socialist Ba'ath Party was founded by Michel Aflaq, a Syrian school teacher in the late 1940s. The party's early slogan, 'unity, freedom, socialism' attracted a generation of Arab nationalists to Aflaq's mystical vision of an Arab renaissance – ba'ath, in Arabic.

Unlike Nasser, who began as an Egyptian nationalist, Aflaq was always a pan-Arabist. For him, Arab unity was the prerequisite for Arab freedom – the defeat of colonialism. In 1963, the Ba'ath Party in Syria and Iraq led successful coups, but the party's pan-Arab organisation quickly fragmented, eventually leaving two rival and hostile factions in power in Baghdad and Damascus.

The weakness of the civilian governments which followed independence had not brought to power their radical critics. Instead, Syria was shaken by a series of military coups and counter-coups, sometimes with the support of the Ba'ath party, and sometimes against it. Unlike the Free Officers in Egypt, none of these military rulers had been able to consolidate their power.

Shukri Quwatli's description of his fellow-countrymen neatly sums up the exasperation felt by conventional politicians at the Syrian love of politics. As he handed power to Nasser following the proclamation of the union he commented: 'You have acquired a nation of politicians; fifty percent believe themselves to be national leaders, twenty-five percent to be prophets, and at least ten percent to be gods.'[127]

The union was precipitated by the army, and not the politicians, however. In January 1958, a group of army officers, led by Chief-of-Staff Afif al-Bizri, flew to Cairo, having declared to the cabinet that the country was in danger of collapse and that the officers were going to Egypt to seek help. The officers' sudden departure revealed that the army, too, feared the growing influence of the Communists, but was too weak and divided to take action itself. Thus the aims of the radical nationalists of the Ba'ath party and the officers appeared to coincide – both feared the continuing weakness of the state would allow the left to gain ground, and neither had confidence in the liberal politicians in the government to do anything about it. '"Do with us what you will", they said in effect to 'Abd-al-Nasser, "only save us from the politicians and from ourselves."'[128]

Nasser, for his part, was at first the reluctant partner in this rushed marriage. The Syrian army was riven by factionalism, while the civilian politicians were also divided. Nasser was undeniably popular in Syria, but it is easy to sustain the aura of a hero from afar – once caught in the maelstrom of Syrian politics, he would find himself in competition with powerful rivals. The Syrian Communist Party was far stronger than its Egyptian counterpart, and the Muslim Brotherhood in Syria had provided a safe haven for Egyptian Islamists persecuted by Nasser. There were practical difficulties also – not least the fact that the two parts of the union were different socially and economically. Syria had a population of 5 million compared to Egypt's 20 million, and the two countries had no common frontier – instead they faced each other across a well-armed enemy: Israel.

On the other hand, the possibilities which union offered were tantalizing. As veteran journalist Patrick Seale puts it, Nasser would have found it difficult to pass by when such an opportunity was given to him. 'Reluctant Abd-al-Nasser may well have been. But he must soon have realized what powerful backing Syria's immolation would give to his own claims to Arab leadership. He would become overnight the heir to all the dreams, hope and patriotic fantasies for which Syria had so long been the focus. After marriage to this most Arab bride of all, there would be no doubting Egypt's Arab destiny.' [129]

In a four-hour meeting with Chief of Staff Afif al-Bizri and Salah-al-Din al-Bitar, Syrian Foreign Minister and a founder of the Ba'ath party, he put forward his conditions for unity. The Syrian political landscape would be reshaped in the Egyptian model. Political parties, including the Ba'ath party, which had been one of the main supporters of the union, would be dissolved, and replaced at a later date by a 'National Union' along the lines of a similar body in Egypt. The officers, far from securing a role at the centre of government, would be expected to return to their barracks and withdraw from politics. Nasser himself would be given complete authority to shape the new unified state.

Although the Ba'ath leadership agreed with Nasser's proposals, there was fierce opposition to the idea from other politicians. The Syrian cabinet drafted a reply to Nasser, envisaging a federal union, which would allow the two countries greater autonomy. Bitar took the proposals back to Cairo on 25 January, but they were rejected by Nasser: the union was to be total, or it would not happen at all. Faced with deadlock, Afif al-Bizri came out strongly in support of total union, reportedly threatening to send those who disagreed to the notorious prison at Mezze. Only the Communists struck a discordant note. On 4 February, three days after the union was proclaimed, Khalid Bakdash left for exile in Eastern Europe and the party returned to the under-ground. Unlike the Ba'ath, who thought that they could dominate the new state from within, the Communists refused to commit political suicide.

Carried away with the passions of the moment, many Syrians seem to have agreed with Bizri. The announcement of unity brought cheering crowds into the streets. The voices of dissenters were swept away. Nasser went to Damascus, and in a speech before the tomb of Salah-al-Din, founder of the Ayyubid dynasty and liberator of Jerusalem from the Crusaders, he pledged *to follow Salah-al-Din's example to realize total Arab unity.*[130]

Revolution in Iraq

While Nasser worked to remake Syrian society in the image of Egypt, events in the outside world continued to move in his favour. In July, only five months after the United Arab Republic was proclaimed, Nasser's greatest rival was swept from power in Iraq by a handful of soldiers, who seemed to be mirror image of the Egyptian Free Officers. Nuri al-Sa'id, prime minister of Iraq and the architect of the Baghdad Pact, was killed in the street as he escaped dressed as a woman, while King Faisal and several members of the royal family were gunned down in the palace. Few Iraqis grieved for them. The streets of Baghdad filled with people celebrating the army coup and the end of the Hashemite dynasty. Armed popular resistance groups, led by the Communists, sprang up to defend the revolution.

The movement which overthrew the Hashemite monarchy in Iraq had deep roots in Iraqi society. As in Egypt, the handful of army officers who dealt the final blow to the old regime on 14 July would not have succeeded without the mass protests which hollowed out the old order, leaving little but a façade of repression in place. Huge waves of protests and strikes in 1948 and 1952 pushed the Iraqi government to rely more and more on brute force to maintain its rule, while the duel between Nasser and the western governments inspired hundreds of thousands of Iraqis to dream of the day they too could be rid of their corrupt and hated rulers.

In the short term, however, the spark for the revolt came from outside. Unity between Egypt and Syria upset Lebanon's fragile political balance. The Lebanese Republic, like Syria, was carved out of the Ottoman Empire by the French at the end of the First World War. To the largely Christian Mount Lebanon area, the mandate authorities added Sunni-dominated Beirut, and the Shi'a villages of the Jabal Amil in the South. The Maronite Christians, long favoured by the French, emerged as the dominant group in the new state, in alliance with the Sunni merchants of Beirut. However, the mandate authorities demographic engineering ensured that the Maronites' grip on power was fragile and open to challenge. The confessional division of executive power was enshrined in the unwritten National Pact of 1943: control of the presidency and the army would go to the Maronites, the prime minister would be a Sunni, the speaker of parliament a Shi'a, while the other sects had to be content with mere ministries.

By 1958, however, this convenient arrangement between the leading families of each sect was beginning to break down. Many young Lebanese were enthusiastic supporters of Arab nationalism, which also found a ready audience among the hundred thousand Palestinian refugees living in Beirut since their expulsion by the Israelis in 1948. Despite Lebanon's formal independence, left-wingers and nationalists saw the Lebanese government's pro-Western policies as a return to colonial rule in another form. Camille Chamoun, the Maronite President, was a fervent opponent of Nasser. In 1957 he had abandoned Lebanon's traditional policy of neutrality to accept the Eisenhower Doctrine.

Union between Egypt and Syria provided the background to a brief but bloody civil war in Lebanon, set off by the assassination of an anti-government newspaper editor. Left-wing and nationalist opponents of Chamoun, including the charismatic Druze leader Kamal Jumblatt, fought Maronite paramilitaries, including the ultra-right Phalange Party. Fu'ad Chehab, commander in chief of the Lebanese Army, held back from intervention, fearing that the army itself would disintegrate into warring factions. Nasser, although sympathetic to Chamoun's opponents, was understandably cautious. He had no desire to embroil Egypt and Syria in a civil war in Lebanon, particularly when the UAR was only a few months old and unity still fragile and untested. After 1956, he also had no illusions about the capacity of either Egyptian or Syrian forces to take on one of the Great Powers.

In January 1957, US President Dwight D. Eisenhower promised to provide military or economic aid to any state which requested US help against 'overt armed aggression from any nation controlled by International Communism.'

The new policy was widely seen as a response to Egypt's arms deal with Czechoslovakia, which had spurred other Arab countries to look to the USSR for support.

Nuri, however, seems to have seen the crisis in Lebanon as an opportunity to reverse the set-back of Egyptian-Syrian unity. Iraq and Jordan had swiftly concluded a royal federation of their own, with Nuri as joint prime minister. In response to Chamoun's appeals for aid, Nuri hinted that Iraq might send troops to Lebanon. His real aim was Syria, however. Previous Iraqi governments had long sought to dominate Syria, and Nuri thought that Syria's embrace with Nasser could be broken. Iraqi troops were given orders to march for northern Jordan. Their commanders thought that Nuri was preparing to invade Syria. In response, two battalions led by Abd-al-Karim Qassim and Abd-al-Salam Aref swept in the opposite direction: into Baghdad to seize the royal palace.

Nasser immediately welcomed the news of Nuri's downfall. He flew to Moscow to consult with Khrushchev, although he failed to gain a promise of Soviet military aid should America move against Iraq. In Lebanon, however, storm clouds were already gathering. As the Hashemite monarchy came crashing down in Baghdad, Camille Chamoun invoked the Eisenhower Doctrine and called on the US to come to his aid. On 15 July startled bikini-clad sunbathers on the beaches of Beirut watched the first of 14,000 US troops splash ashore.

Back in Damascus, Nasser warned that the days of colonial occupation were over. *We see today a threat unleashed by the imperialist powers. We see today America occupying Lebanon and Britain occupying Jordan. I say to them in your name: 'there was an occupation in the past. There was the French occupation of Damascus and the British occupation of Baghdad and Cairo and Amman. Where are they now?' Their occupation ended, it turned to dust.* [131]

Seeds of defeat

Despite Nasser's fears that the landings by US Marines in Beirut in July 1958 heralded a new era of foreign intervention in the Middle East, the invasion never came. The Lebanese conflict was brought to an end with the election of General Fu'ad Chehab to the presidency and the Marines went home. Britain did not lift a finger to avenge the Iraqi royal family, while the US left Iraq's new republican leaders in peace.

But even as the threat of foreign intervention receded, cracks began to appear in the facade of Arab unity. Despite, or more likely because of, the similarity between the two leaders of the Free Officers in Egypt and Iraq, the relations between Qassim and Nasser soured quickly. Qassim was unenthusiastic about proposals for Iraq to join the UAR. He may have seen the Egyptian leader's popularity as a threat to his own position. On the morning of the Iraqi revolution, crowds in Baghdad could be heard chanting 'we are your soldiers, Gamal Abd-al-Nasser' over the radio.[132]

Quite apart from his distaste for playing second fiddle to Nasser, Qassim had other grounds for caution. Iraq did not only face west, towards the Arab world. The Shi'a of central and southern Iraq had strong cultural and religious links to Iran. The Kurds of the north were suspicious of Arab nationalism. Qassim himself, son of a Sunni Arab father and Shi'a Kurdish mother, was a living symbol of Iraq's diverse heritage. By the end of summer 1958 Qassim had 'thrown his weight on the side of particularism and become the centre of its hopes, even if he went on asserting that he was "above trends and inclinations".'[133]

In this he was supported by the Communists, who emerged from the revolution of July 1958 better organised than their comrades in Syria and Egypt. The Iraqi Communist Party, although formally supportive of the idea of greater Arab unity against 'imperialism', was resolutely opposed to union on the conditions Nasser had imposed on Syria: the dissolution of all political parties.

Meanwhile, both the Iraqi and Syrian Ba'ath parties were pushing for unity between the UAR and Iraq. The Iraqi party, although smaller than the Communist Party, had won hundreds of new members and supporters by campaigning for unity. A favourite rhyming slogan invoked Nasser's name and his dark complexion: 'al-wahdah bakir, bakir ma'-il-asmar abd-al-nasir' ('unity tomorrow, tomorrow, with the brown Abd-al-Nasser').[134] By adopting Nasser as a symbol of unity, the Iraqi Ba'ath party hoped to find a balance to the growing power of the Communists, who were fast becoming Abd-al-Karim Qassim's most fervent partisans. The Syrian Ba'ath also had great hopes of unity between Iraq and the UAR. Iraq's addition to the union would completely alter the balance of power within the UAR. Syria and Iraq combined would present a formidable demographic, economic and political counterweight to the dominance of Egypt and Nasser.

The standard view is that Nasser's own feelings about the campaign for unity were more measured. He met Abd-al-Salam Aref, Qassim's co-conspirator in the Free Officers and vice-president of the new republic, in Damascus on 18 July, just four days after the overthrow of the monarchy. According to Aref's memoirs, when he raised the question of unity, Nasser told him that the revolution needed to consolidate itself first.[135] Despite this, Aref became Nasser's most high-profile supporter in Iraq and began to call publicly for Iraq to join the UAR. Said Aburish argues that

Nasser was eager to bring Iraq into the UAR, and even asked for permission to land in Baghdad as he flew back from Moscow, only to be rebuffed by Qassim. According to Aburish, it was only after this rejection that Aref met Nasser in Damascus.[136]

Aref's star quickly waned. He fell out with Qassim, was accused of treason and narrowly escaped execution. By March 1959 Nasser had been persuaded to support an attempt to over-throw Qassim from outside, through a coup led by dissident Iraqi officers in the garrison of Mosul, supported by UAR forces over the border in Syria. The rebellion failed: the Communists, the regular Iraqi army, and Kurdish peasants crushed the insurgents. Nasser's attacks on Qassim became ever more personal; he made great use of a pun on Qassim's name, calling him the *Divider of Iraq*. He accused the Iraqi leader of not only conspiring with the Communists against him, but also of *following the example of Nuri al-Sa'id, and the example of the enemies of Arab nationalism.*[137]

The battle with the Communists

The rise of the Iraqi Communists gave new hope to their Syrian comrades. In February the Communists' leaders had fled to the Soviet Union while those who remained behind burnt the party's membership lists and prepared to go underground. Qassim and Aref's coup in July prompted Khalid Bakdash, the party leader, to draw up a new programme. He challenged Nasser to allow free elections within the UAR and to introduce democratic freedoms. In response, Nasser launched a vitriolic attack on the Syrian Communists, accusing them of *rejecting Arab nationalism and Arab unity* and of being *stooges of imperialism and Zionism*.[138] Hundreds of members of the Syrian Communist Party were arrested and the party dissolved. Meanwhile the UAR's state-controlled media continued to denounce the Communists. In Egypt, too, the Communists also faced repression, although they, unlike their comrades in Syria, supported Nasser and backed the UAR.

Between December 1958 and April 1959 nearly 1000 party members and supporters were arrested. Many were tortured and at least nine died in prison as a result.

Nasser's opposition to Communism was not a new development. He believed that the Communists were wrong to divide the nation against itself by raising slogans of class war. Instead, a strategy of national development would provide the means to end economic and social inequality. Already by 1954 he had become an accomplished anti-Communist polemicist. He told a meeting of trade unionists in April 1954 that he had once met Bindari Pasha, who Nasser described as *the Red Pasha* and a leading Communist. *I went round to his place. And I said to him 'look mate, all this talk about raising workers' and peasants' living standards, it's great, but how are you going to do it?' . . . We've heard it all before, brothers. To raise the peasants' living standards and raise the workers' living standards we have to increase the wealth of this country. The cash you take home reflects the national wealth divided up between us. What the individual gets won't go up unless the whole lot increases. And we won't increase the national wealth unless we work at it. We'll have to get agriculture working and get industry working. Anyone who tells you anything different is having a laugh at your expense.*[139]

As the task of increasing the national wealth proved difficult by free-market methods alone, Nasser moved towards state intervention, and despite his attempts to maintain a balance between the two superpowers, towards closer relations with the USSR. Nasser's attitude to the Soviet Union remained complex and ambivalent. At the same time as he was persecuting the Egyptian and Syrian Communists, he accepted increasing amounts of Soviet aid, including a loan to build the High Dam. In part Nasser's attack on the Communists was motivated by political considerations. The Communist Party was a potential rival among the very groups Nasser had attempted to woo with his reforms: the working class and the peasants. But also at an economic level Nasser was determined not to fall into the trap of dependency on the Soviet Union. He perceived that Soviet 'advisers', whether economic or military, might prove as difficult to get rid of as their British predecessors had been.

In 1959 there were also immediate political concerns. The failure of the Mosul uprising in Iraq, defeated largely thanks to a huge mobilisation by the Iraqi Communists, pushed Nasser onto the attack against the party's patrons in Moscow. He quarrelled publicly with Khrushchev, attacking the Soviet leader for what he described as interference in the UAR's internal affairs. Before a huge crowd in Damascus, a few days after events in Mosul, he attacked Syrian and Iraqi Communists. *Whether the conspiracies originate abroad, or whether the Communists go from Damascus to Baghdad to organise a plot against their native land, we know, oh my brothers, that the conspiracy by the Communists against our country will not succeed. Whoever betrays his country, whoever is prepared to work as a foreign agent . . . this, oh my brothers is the nature of collaborators, who are prepared to sell our homeland at any price.*[140]

Development or dependency?

Apart from a small number of essentially political economic reforms – in particular the Land Reform of 1952 – the Free Officers did not, in the early years, attempt to direct the economy centrally. The officers' own ideas on economics reflected the mixture of ideological influences which had shaped their movement. This did translate into a general hostility to foreign capital, and a strong notion of the need for development to benefit a broader cross-section of society, but was not a worked-out plan for sweeping economic change.

Apart from the Land Reform, the impetus towards state-led development was driven by outside events. Thus the nationalisation of the Suez Canal, described as a mechanism by which to produce the funds to build the Aswan Dam, was in reality a political act. In the event, the USSR provided funding for the Dam, not the nationalised Canal. But the fact of nationalisation and the cost of the war which followed also had their economic consequences. One of these was Nasser's decision to expel British and French nationals and the sequestration of their property, which took place during the crisis. The war accelerated a process which had been gathering pace for around twenty years: the Egyptianisation of the economy. For many years foreign capital dominated manufacturing and trade in Egypt. French and British firms controlled large parts of the cotton industry, where Egypt was just a small cog in the great imperial economies of Europe. By the 1940s the balance was shifting towards greater Egyptian ownership.

This shift, however, did not produce the levels of economic growth needed to industrialise Egypt. The Free Officers, like many of their contemporaries, saw one of the principal problems to be the dominance of the landed elite – the 'feudalists' targeted by the land reform. The great landowners were seen as a block to development and progress, as they were reluctant to release the wealth locked up in their estates to invest in industry. Gradually it became clear that without massive state intervention, Egypt would never achieve the levels of investment necessary for industrial take-off. The state could act as a lever to prise open opportunities for international finance – from either the Western or Eastern powers. The state had the legal and physical means to force a change of direction on the economy; to plan and centralise Egypt's meagre resources.

Between 1952 and 1957, government intervention in the Egyptian economy was restricted to Land Reform, the establishment of state co-operatives in agriculture, investment in selected heavy industries, such as steel, planning for large scale investment projects such as the High Dam, and the expansion of education and welfare provision. However, after the war in 1956, the process of state intervention deepened with the nationalisation of all the banks, the establishment of the Economic Organism, which was created to administer the property and enterprises seized from British and French owners during 1956, and the evolution of a comprehensive planning system. The period 1957-60 saw the emergence of a mixed economy, with the state sector growing in importance. After 1961 the economy saw rapid change, as waves of nationalisations and punitive sequestrations brought most of modern industry, large department stores, financial institutions, building and transport firms into the public sector. Government control of agriculture was extended through the expansion of the cooperative system. Although some land, urban real estate and most small businesses remained in private hands, most of Egypt's economy was now state-controlled. The Socialist Laws granted new rights to workers and employment in public administration increased.

This rapid change in Egypt's economic structure seemed, at least for a while, to bring startling rates of growth. The economy grew quickly after 1959, averaging 6.4-6.6 percent per year between 1959/60 and 1964/65, up from an average of 4.7 percent per year between 1945 and 1952.[141] Manufacturing output grew even more quickly, in 1960/1 rising by 15.5 percent per year, and remaining over 10 percent per year until 1963/4.[142] The sudden turn towards state ownership surprised many and alarmed some.

More than any other development project, the High Dam was associated with Nasser. Although he risked war with Britain and France for the sake of the Dam, by nationalizing the Suez Canal, the project was actually financed largely by Soviet loans. The first agreement was signed in 1958 and the second in 1960.

Nasser lived to see the initial phase of the project completed in 1964, and the opening of the Dam's power generation plant in 1967. It was left to Anwar Sadat to mark the completion of Nasser's plan in January 1971.

The High Dam is over 3.5 km long, and rises 111 metres above the bed of the Nile. The river waters have created a vast lake, Lake Nasser, 500 km long.

A key figure in the move towards state planning was Aziz Sidqi, a young economist who was appointed to run the Tahrir Province, a desert reclamation scheme. Doreen Warriner visited the province's cooperative farms in the mid-1950s. She noted that the children were 'magnificently healthy' in this highly regimented experiment in social engineering: 'The contrast with Iraq is complete. There money for dams is available and to spare, and foreign firms are doing the work, which will bring the new water supplies forward. But unless things change, the water and the land will be used to grow poor barley crops with half-starved labour. Egypt, on the other hand, has set its human values first, and gets the men and women and the land ready for the water, while raising funds and the whirlwind by playing Great Power politics.' [143]

Although the Tahrir experiment later ran into difficulties, Sidqi continued to rise within the administration, becoming Minister of Industry in 1956. He enjoyed a close relationship with Nasser at this period, and was one of the few who won his confidence. The five-year plan which was announced in 1957 was largely Sidqi's work. Although the plan relied heavily on private financing, Sidqi was convinced that the state had to take a strong line to force private investors to provide the money needed for development. Nasser too was carried along by a sense of urgency; announcing in December 1958 that the five-year plan would be completed in three. *We have to work twice as fast, once for the hundred years of backwardness that have passed, once to provide work for the 350,000 persons who are born to us each year.* [144]

As the nationalisations gathered pace, divisions began to appear. The July Decrees of 1961 brought a large part of the non-agricultural sector under state control. Law 117 nationalized the remaining private banks, fifty shipping companies and firms in heavy industries. Law 118 obliged a number of private companies to sell 50 percent of their shares to the government. In Syria, where the public sector was even smaller than Egypt, and where private sector interests were better organised politically, the socialist decrees triggered the coup which led to the dissolution of the UAR in September 1961.

Nasser, fearing that a similar movement could appear in Egypt, moved quickly against those individuals he described as *reactionaries working with imperialism*.[145] In October 1961, the property of 167 people was sequestrated, and they were deprived of their political rights. 'The names of those initially sanctioned were given wide publicity and read like the honour roll of Egypt's pre-war bourgeoisie.'[146] Now the revolution entered what John Waterbury describes as its 'self-consciously socialist phase'.[147] Incomes above £E 10,000 were taxed at 90 percent. Public sector directors could not earn more than £E 5,000 as their basic salary, nor occupy more than one public post. 15 percent of joint stock company profits had to go towards workers' housing and community projects, while workers and clerical staff were guaranteed a seat on the company board of directors. New laws reduced the working week, and set a minimum wage.

Aziz Sidqi described later that one day after lunch with Nasser in May 1961, he saw a copy of his ministry's *Dalil al-Sina't*, an inventory of Egyptian industry on the President's desk. 'Nasser then asked how the state could plan anything if the industrial sector was under the control of "individuals". Sidqi saw that Nasser had marked various companies with a lead pencil and that was that.'[148] Some analysts have argued that Nasser's decision to carry out the July Decrees was motivated more by political than economic goals – the further concentration of power in the state, and thus in his own hands. [149] The improvised and almost conspiratorial nature of the decision seems to fit this analysis. Nasser was known for both his suspicion and his single-mindedness.

Although the July Decrees may well have expressed Nasser's personal frustrations, they also reflected a growing sense among a layer of technocrats and public managers that without decisive action from above Egypt would never industrialise. The first Five Year Plan, which was begun in 1960, set ambitious targets for production, investment and saving. Yet state officials felt that private enterprise was dragging its feet. An editorial in *Bourse égyptienne* in 1960 noted: 'attempts to secure co-operation from the over-privileged business group had failed.'[150] As Raymond Hinnebusch puts it 'it appears Nasser finally decided that if the bourgeoisie would not invest, the state would seize its economic assets and invest the profits itself in the sectors it considered crucial.'[151]

Nasser used his authority as President to push through the new direction, which was not shared by the majority of his colleagues among the leading Free Officers. But he could count on the support of the 'second circle' of the Free Officers and civilian technocrats, who came to dominate economic decision-making during the 1960s. As economic change accelerated, Nasser's isolation from his old comrades became clearer. Abd-al-Latif al-Bughdadi, one of the core of the Free Officers since the early days, resigned from the Presidential Council in 1964.

In the early 1960s Nasser was not alone in pushing for a greater role for the state in the economy. Across large parts of Africa, Asia and the Middle East other Third World leaders also experimented with state capitalism. The prize was the astonishing levels of development which the USSR appeared to have achieved. Once a poor, backward country, the Soviet Union had made itself a superpower through the use of planning and state-led industrialisation and the forced collectivisation of agriculture. This vision of the future attracted many leaders, who were not Communists, but nationalists who had emerged from the victorious national liberation movements.

And despite his ferocious attacks on 'Western imperialism' Nasser did not want to shut the door to American aid. In 1961 Egypt sought a $150 m loan from the International Monetary

Fund, and accepted the delivery of 200,000 tons of American wheat. The supply of US food aid was also a sign that rising rates of growth had not solved all of Egypt's economic problems. The economy was still highly dependent on a single crop: cotton. Cotton worm destroyed around half the 1961 crop, depriving Egypt of vital foreign exchange revenue. Nasser also corresponded with US President Kennedy, inviting him to send some of his closest advisers to see for themselves the difficulties he faced in trying to develop Egypt. In 1962 Kennedy sent his economics adviser Dr Edward Mason to Cairo for a series of meetings with Nasser.

The collapse of the UAR

If the trigger for the collapse of union with Syria was the Socialist Decrees of 1961, the roots of the crisis went much deeper. Tabitha Petran, writing a few years after the union fell apart, paints a picture of an imposed Egyptian bureaucracy attempting to milk the Syrian economy for the benefit of Egyptian firms while Nasser's police and security services crushed dissent and rigged elections. 'No less than four secret police networks operated in Syria. The ordinary citizen walked in fear of a legion of secret agents. His mail was censored, his telephone tapped, his conversations reported, his comings and goings watched.'[152] Although one-sided, her account gives a sense of the bitterness many Syrians felt at the failure of the union.

For his part, Nasser had a different explanation. On 16 October 1961, after the collapse of the UAR, he admitted that mistakes had been made. *We must have the courage to confess our errors: we must blame ourselves for the collapse of the union with Syria.*[153] The problem, he believed, was that he had been too ready to compromise with *reactionaries* who had stabbed him in the back - the rich and powerful landowners who opposed land reform and Syria's capitalists who dreaded the extension of Egypt's programme of nationalisations. Nasser could point to the behaviour of the conservative politicians who formed a government following Syria's secession. One of their first acts was to vote themselves a 333 percent pay rise. The landlords, for their part, set about expelling peasant farmers and taking back their old properties.

Reality was more complex than either of these caricatures. In creating the UAR Nasser, the Syrian generals and the Ba'ath party had to turn the slogans of Arab unity into a functioning economic and political system. From the start, Nasser attempted to use his immense personal prestige as a lever to push Syria's economy and society down the road Egypt had been travelling since 1952. He was also prepared to expend Egypt's resources to speed up this process. Despite later complaints of 'Egyptian colonisation', Egypt made up deficits in the Syrian budget and provided financial aid to the UAR's 'Northern Region', as Syria was now known.

As Robert Heydemann explains, the collapse of the UAR was about a lot more than Syrian dislike of Egyptian bureaucracy and red tape. It was also a result of 'the efforts of the Egyptian authorities to impose a distinctive developmental model that was populist, industrializing and authoritarian in character and organised along rigidly corporatist lines.' [154] And one of Nasser's greatest problems was his mistrust of the potential Syrian allies who could help him achieve such a radical transformation.

The Ba'athists had expected to be rewarded with a dominant position in the political structures of the UAR. They were quickly disillusioned. The party's leaders were shunted into largely ceremonial positions in Cairo, while the real power remained in the hands of Nasser's men. Although Nasser attacked their left-wing competitors, the Communists, he also gave free rein to their rivals on the right. In summer 1959 elections to the 'National Union' – newly-extended to Syria – were a disaster for the Ba'ath. Out of more than 9,000 seats contested at local level in Syria the party only won around 250.

The National Union, which Nasser had set up in Egypt in 1957, was not a political party. Like its predecessor, the Liberation Rally, the union was conceived as a structure which would simultaneously represent and mobilise the whole of society. Nasser explained the body's aims in an article in the daily *Al-Ahram* in July 1959: *'The National Union is one means for us to enforce our internal conditions and the necessities of our foreign policy. It is the cadre through which we will realize our revolution, for the security of the homeland and to safeguard its independence. It is a form of peaceful coexistence between the social classes.'*[155]

Nasser's emphasis on the 'peaceful coexistence' between social classes was not accidental. He sought to perform a difficult balancing act: on the one hand he brought the trade unions under state control and neutralised the left through repression, while on the other he tried to subordinate private capital to the state. In Egypt the equation worked: Nasser broke the political and economic power of the landlords and then the private sector bourgeoisie, and transferred their resources to the state. Some of this wealth then trickled back down to Egypt's workers and fellahin through welfare schemes, rent controls and bonuses, but the vast bulk of it was mobilised for economic development.

In Syria the balancing act broke down. Nasser neutralised the left, and after a long struggle even gained control of the unruly Syrian trade union movement. To do this, he tended to lean towards the private sector and the liberal and conservative politicians, which represented its interests. He attempted to split the unity of the Syrian bourgeoisie by forcing through land reform while courting businessmen. However, when it came to enforcing the domination of the state over the private sector through the Socialist Decrees of 1961, he faced a well-organised revolt. Army officers opposed to the union seized power in Damascus, then handed power over to a civilian government of conservative politicians. There was little support in Syria for the UAR. The Ba'ath had withdrawn from the government in 1959 in protest at being excluded from real power. The party was split and disorientated. Despite the cheering crowds which had welcomed him whenever he visited, all Nasser's prestige had been able to do in Syria was to create the façade and not the substance of union.

Yemen

The collapse of the UAR reflected in an extreme form the deep fissures which had appeared in the project of Arab unity. Egypt's intervention in Yemen began partly as an attempt to revive this dream, but ended up deepening the divisions in the Arab world. Egyptian troops became embroiled in a bloody civil war and the intervention brought Nasser into conflict with Saudi Arabia.

African anti-colonial movements found financial and diplomatic backing in Cairo. Leaders of newly independent African nations, like Kwame Nkrumah in Ghana and Patrice Lumumba in the Congo shared Nasser's vision of an international struggle against colonialism. Egypt's battles to achieve economic independence were also mirrored in many African countries. Nasser dammed the Nile and Nkrumah dammed the Volta.

Nasser also intervened to protect the families of his allies. After Lumumba's assassination following his overthrow by Mobutu Sese Seku, his wife and children found a new home in Cairo.

On the face of it, Yemen seemed an unlikely candidate for an Egyptian-style revolution in 1962. The country was divided between the ancient Zaydi Shi'a theocracy ruled by Imam Ahmad from San'aa in the north, and a British protectorate in the port-city of Aden in the south. British influence over the Gulf kingdoms remained strong, and Aden was seen by British governments as a crucial foothold in Arabia, in addition to its role as a staging post on the way to India and beyond.

Imam Ahmad, an absolute monarch, had been an unusual partner in Nasser's plans for Arab unity. The Imamate joined the

UAR in a loose federation called the Union of Arab States in 1958, although unity was never much more than an agreement on paper. The UAS was dissolved following the collapse of the UAR. Imam Ahmad had become increasingly worried by Nasser's turn towards socialism, which he denounced as 'ungodly' in a poem broadcast in December 1961.[156] Discontent with the Imamate became open rebellion the following year. Despite Imam Ahmad's attempts to secure Egyptian support through the link with UAR, a growing urban middle class was becoming increasingly impatient for political and social change. The Imam still ruled as a medieval monarch – he had two of his brothers beheaded in 1955 for their part in an attempt to overthrow him.

When Imam Ahmad died in September 1962, republicans seized their chance and rebelled against his son, Muhammad al-Badr. On 27 September, Abdallah al-Sallal, the chief of staff and formerly one of the new Imam's closest aides, joined an artillery bombardment of the royal palace. The following day al-Sallal announced the formation of a revolutionary government and proclaimed the Yemen Arab Republic. The UAR and the Communist bloc countries recognized the new government, followed by the USA in December 1962. However it quickly became clear that the Imam, who the rebels initially claimed to have killed, was still alive and receiving increasing support from Saudi Arabia. Nasser dispatched Egyptian troops to Yemen to prop up the new government on 6 October, but were unable to defeat the Saudi-backed royalist forces which maintained control of around a third of the country.

As the war dragged on, Yemenis came to resent the Egyptian presence, despite Nasser's attempts to foster economic development as well as offering military support. In particular, close Egyptian control of the new republic's political leadership made Nasser many enemies. By 1963 Egypt had 15,000 troops in Yemen, and the republicans were no closer to crushing the royalists. The war became increasingly brutal on both sides, Egyptian planes carried out gas attacks on Yemeni villages, while the royalist forces mutilated their prisoners. Nasser also channelled arms to nationalists fighting for independence for Aden, which was then still under British rule.

The ghosts of unity

February and March 1963 brought a sudden reversal of fortune for Nasser. On 8 February the Ba'ath seized power in Baghdad, killing Nasser's old rival, Abd-al-Karim Qassim, and launching a vicious crackdown on the Communists. Exactly a month later, the Syrian Ba'athists took control of Damascus. Nasser immediately cabled his support. In the words of Malcolm Kerr, 'his refusal to compromise with reactionaries and separatists in the Arab world had seemingly been vindicated, and the road to a revived and expanded Arab union was open.'

In June delegations from Iraq, Syria and Egypt met in Cairo for lengthy discussions on the issue of unity. However, the bitter experience of the union between Syria and Egypt had sown the seeds of mutual mistrust. Both sides had reason to feel aggrieved. The Ba'ath still needed Nasser as a symbol of Arab nationalism, but feared that he would once again exclude them from power. Nasser did not believe that the Ba'ath regimes in either Syria or Iraq were stable enough to take the risk of hitching Egypt's fortunes to another union.

Nasser appears to have over-awed his opponents. The transcript of the meetings, which the Egyptian government later published, shows him dominating the talks: he could persuade, cajole, bully or joke with equal ease. The Syrian and Iraqi delegates had none of his self-assurance. 'To them he was "Mr President" or "Your Excellency"; he called them by their first names'.[157] At one point, Nasser enquired who was ruling Syria. Rashid Qutayni of the Syrian Ba'ath party explained that a 'Revolutionary Council' of ten officers and ten civilians had been appointed. *'That won't do at all,*

Rashid said Nasser. *Give me the details.* Qutayni mumbled evasively. *What I want to know is, who is on this council with which we're supposed to contract a union. Am I to deal with ghosts?'* [158]

As the talks dragged on, hopes of another Arab union withered. With the collapse of the UAR only two years previously, the moment for unity appeared to have passed.

Development in crisis

By 1965 Nasser was preoccupied with other problems at home. The Socialist Decrees of July 1961 and the nationalisations which followed had brought most of the Egyptian economy under state control. However the ambitious plans for development of new industries proved difficult to realise. Poor planning meant that expensive machinery and materials lay idle, while Egypt was importing basic foodstuffs in increasingly large quantities.[159] A severe balance-of-payments deficit forced Nasser to run down Egypt's foreign currency reserves to pay for the imports needed to keep the industrial development programme running.

There were shortages of basic goods, the black market flourished. Smugglers, known as *tuggar al-shanta* (bag merchants) made small fortunes by travelling abroad as tourists and returning with suitcases stuffed with consumer goods. This was the other side of the state capitalist model of development, familiar across the Eastern Bloc. And just as in the Soviet world, those at the helm of the state did not go short. People began to grumble about the former Free Officers and the public sector bourgeoisie, now linked to the landed elite by marriage and a shared affluent lifestyle. Instead of reallocating resources, indirect taxation was used by the government in an increasingly desperate attempt to raise revenue. The cost of living rose by ten percent in a single year. Discontent turned into open protests as prices rose and working hours were lengthened again. There were demonstrations in the towns of the Delta in 1965 and a rash of strikes in 1966.

The countdown to war

While hopes of Arab unity rose and fell, one issue remained a constant source of tension. Since 1948, hundreds of thousands of Palestinian refugees had been waiting to return to the homes they had been forced to leave when the State of Israel was founded. By the 1960s a new generation was growing up, one which had known nothing but the squalid refugee camps of Gaza, Amman and Beirut. More impatient, and perhaps more desperate than their parents, these young men and women also had less time for the promises of the established Arab leaders, Nasser included, that the liberation of Palestine could only be achieved through the realisation of Arab unity. They contrasted the high-flown rhetoric of the summit meetings with the lack of progress in winning back their homeland. Some looked to the example of Algeria, where a guerrilla war and popular uprising had defeated French colonialism. Others were inspired by the teachings of Mao, and thought that the time was ripe for a revolutionary war of liberation.

During the late 1950s a nucleus of like-minded refugee activists living in the Gulf crystallized around the principle of 'Palestine first'. Liberation of Palestine was the first goal and Arab unity only a secondary consideration. At some point in the early 1960s these activists adopted the name Palestinian National Liberation Movement, better known as Fatah, from the reversal of the group's Arabic acronym.

By the mid 1960s these two different approaches could be tested out in practice. In January 1964, Nasser persuaded 13 Arab kings, presidents and emirs to meet in Cairo to discuss plans by Israel to divert water from the Sea of Galilee to the Negev desert. The conference appointed Ahmad al-Shuqairi, a Palestinian diplomat at the Arab League, to set up a new body which aimed at 'organising the Palestinian people and enabling them to play their role in the liberation of their country and their self-determination.'[160] Shuqairi, who was well-known for his overblown oratory, steered the newly-born Palestine Liberation Organisation (PLO) into controversy within a few months of its founding. In July 1964 he made a statement on behalf of the PLO claiming the whole of the East Bank of the Jordan for a future Palestinian state, much to the consternation of his Jordanian hosts.

Fatah's activists along with many of the other Palestinian radical nationalists were unimpressed by both the PLO and Shuqairi, whom they saw as Nasser's man. They were determined to launch independent Palestinian military action against Israel but found the PLO's armed wing, the Palestinian Liberation Army, was tightly controlled by the states which had founded it. Although he understood the value of guerrilla warfare as a military strategy and had used it as a bargaining tool during negotiations to secure British withdrawal from the Canal Zone, Nasser was desperate to avoid being drawn into a premature confrontation. In 1965 he responded sharply to Palestinian calls for Egypt to move against Israel. *Is it not essential to have a plan? If Israeli aggression takes place against Syria, do I attack Israel? That would mean that Israel is the one to determine the battle for me. It hits a tractor or two to force me to move, is this a wise way? It is we who must determine the battle.*[161]

Nasser also hoped to remain in political control of the Palestinian issue. Despite his verbal support for the Palestinian cause and the launch of the PLO, independent Palestinian activists found their room for manoeuvre tightly constrained in Egypt. Ironically, Fatah's founders moved from Cairo, the capital of Arab nationalism, to the conservative monarchies of the Gulf, not only because they needed money and found good jobs there in the construction industry, but also because they found it easier to build a political organisation away from the attentions of Nasser's secret police. In this desire to control the Palestinian movement, Nasser was far from being alone. All the Arab states placed severe restrictions on Palestinian political organisation and frequently denied Palestinians rights to housing, employment and travel on the same basis as their own citizens.

Despite these difficulties, Fatah's commandos launched their first raid on 31 December 1964. Although the actual impact on Israel was minimal – many of the guerrillas were arrested by the Egyptian police in Gaza before they could strike – other operations soon followed. By the end of 1965 Fatah, working under the name *Al-Asifah* (The Storm), claimed 39 separate raids.

While Nasser argued for caution, the Palestinian commandos found a more sympathetic audience in Syria. In February 1966 another coup brought a new group of Ba'athist activists to power. Soon the new government was calling for a 'popular liberation war' to liberate Palestine and rid the Middle East of imperialism and reaction. The new regime also strengthened Syria's links to the Soviet Union, prompting King Hussein of Jordan to raise the spectre of a Soviet-Syrian-Egyptian axis threatening Western interests in the Middle East. The Ba'ath's bravado soon found its echo in Israel and a war of words developed between Tel Aviv and Damascus. The Israelis accused Syria of threatening their water supplies by diverting the Banias River and of sponsoring Palestinian guerrilla raids into Israel from the Golan Heights.

By early 1967, however, the tension seemed to have eased a little. Joint Syrian-Israeli Mixed Armistice Commission talks had broken down, but guerrilla raids began to tail off. The Ba'ath's internal critics, including the Muslim Brotherhood, began to claim the government lacked the stomach for a 'popular liberation war' after all. Then in April, Israel announced a plan to bring the whole of the demilitarised zone between the Syrian and Israeli front lines into cultivation. For the Syrians, this was a deliberate provocation: the open annexation of Arab land. After an armoured Israeli tractor appeared on the disputed land on 7 April, the Syrians launched a mortar attack from their positions on the Golan Heights. The Israelis hit back with tanks and artillery, while their fighter jets pounded Syrian positions with napalm and high explosives. The Syrians lost six planes and around 100 casualties.

It was in this charged atmosphere that reports reached Cairo of massive Israeli troop movements near the Syrian border. To the worried officials in the Foreign Ministry it appeared that the pieces of an Israeli plan to overthrow the Ba'ath regime were falling into place before their eyes. On 11 May Arab listening stations picked up a broadcast on Israel Radio in which General Yitzhak Rabin was heard to declare: 'the moment is coming when we will march on Damascus to overthrow the Syrian Government, because it seems that only military operations can discourage the plans for a people's war with which they threaten us.'[162] Two days later, Dimitri Pojidaev, Soviet Ambassador in Cairo, met Ahmad Hassan al-Fiqi, Under Secretary of Foreign Affairs, and passed him a report providing details of the Israeli mobilisation. To underscore the importance of the message, Soviet President Nikolai Podgorny passed the same information to Anwar Sadat, who was passing through Moscow on the same day.[163]

Denials by the Israelis and the UN forces monitoring the ceasefire lines failed to convince Nasser. Two battalions set off for Sinai the following day. He also demanded the withdrawal of UN forces from the peninsula. On 23 May he ordered the closure of the Gulf of Aqaba to Israeli shipping. In a defiant speech at Bir Gafgafa the previous day he laid down his challenge. *We say they are welcome to war, we are ready for it; our armed forces, our people, all of us are ready for war, but under no circumstances shall we abandon any of our rights. These are our waters.*[164]

To the brink and back

At around 8.30 a.m. on 5 June Field Marshal Abd-al-Hakim Amer's plane took off for a tour of inspection of Egyptian positions in Sinai. Egyptian gunners were given strict instructions not to open fire while the commander-in-chief was airborne. Minutes later, the first wave of Israeli attacks began. While Amer was marooned in the air over Sinai, Israeli fighters hit hundreds of Egyptian aircraft. By the time he landed an hour and a half later 264 combat places had been destroyed, the majority of them incinerated on the runway. All sixteen Egyptian radar stations in Sinai were also out of action by the end of the day.

Israeli Ambassador to the UN Abba Eban woke the Security Council President at 3.10 a.m. New York time to inform him that Israel had acted in self-defence. 'Since the early hours of this morning fierce fighting has broken out between Egyptian air and armoured forces, which moved against Israel, and our forces, which went into action to contain them.' [165] In fact, Israeli commanders had obliterated the Egyptian Air Force, and removed whatever military threat Egypt might have posed to Israel in the first hour of the war. They kept silent about the scale of their victory, however, while Voice of the Arabs filled the airwaves with rumours of significant Israeli losses.

The following day the Gaza Strip, home to hundreds of thousands of Palestinian refugees, fell to Israeli troops. They took Bethlehem and Hebron in the West Bank from the Jordanian army, which had entered the conflict on Egypt's side. Israeli paratroopers fought their way through the narrow streets of East Jerusalem, capturing the Old City including the Al-Aqsa Mosque and the Wailing Wall on 7 June. The Israelis also launched their forces into Sinai. Just as in 1956, they quickly pushed back Egyptian troops towards the Canal. However, unlike 1956, Egypt was not the only object of the Israeli advance. For the Palestinians of the West Bank, 1967 was a repeat of the catastrophe of 1948. Thousands fled across the river towards Amman to swell the miserable refugee camps in the Jordanian capital.

The crisis brought a sudden revival of Arab unity as Nasser accused the US and Britain of sending fighter planes to join the Israeli assault. *British aircraft raided positions on the Syrian and Egyptian fronts in broad daylight ... the enemy was operating with an*

Film star Faten Hamama raises money to rebuild the shattered Egypt, 1967

air force three times stronger than normal,[166] he said later. King Hussein of Jordan had concluded a mutual defence pact with the UAR only hours before the outbreak of war. He faced a stark choice: throw his lot in with Nasser and risk losing the West Bank, or remain neutral and risk losing his throne to a pro-Nasser revolt. He found himself transformed overnight from a British stooge to a defender of Arab nationalism, but Jordanian forces were no match for the Israeli army. Now even the conservative monarchs of the Gulf, Nasser's bitter enemies, promised support as Egypt came under attack. King Faisal of Saudi Arabia followed Iraq's lead and announced an oil boycott of Western governments.

Known affectionately as *Al-Sitt* – the lady – Umm Kulthum was a country girl whose voice first captivated Cairo audiences under the monarchy.

She initially faced a ban from Egypt's airwaves after the Free Officers took power, but it was Nasser who reversed the decision and Umm Kulthum became an icon of the new regime. After Egypt's defeat by Israel in 1967, she withdrew to her villa in Zamalek, but soon changed her mind, throwing herself into a marathon round of concerts to raise money to rebuild Egypt's shattered army.

Umm Kulthum – Star of the Orient – became one of Arab nationalism's most enduring cultural symbols. Her funeral in 1975 drew around 4 million mourners.

On 4 June, the day before the outbreak of war, Nasser had welcomed the participation of Iraq in the mutual defence pact he signed with King Hussein of Jordan: *The Arabs are one nation. In times of stress and times of battle, there is no difference between an Iraqi Arab and an Egyptian Arab and a Jordanian Arab.*[167] Now, as he saw Israeli fighters flying unchallenged over Cairo, Nasser knew that in reality a defeat for Egypt was a defeat for all the Arabs. He cabled Syrian commanders urging them to save their forces from defeat and accept the UN-sponsored ceasefire. An Egyptian counter-attack failed, the army was in chaos and the retreat

Moshe Dayan, walking around the Old City in Jerusalem, 1967

became a rout. Thousands of Egyptian troops were trapped in Sinai behind enemy lines. Nasser's warning to the Syrians came too late. Although the Syrian government asked for a ceasefire at 3.20 am on the morning of 9 June, Israeli commanders launched their assault eight hours later. Israeli forces advanced towards Damascus, taking the Golan Heights overlooking the Sea of Galilee. The Israeli army halted at the town of Qunaitra and accepted the ceasefire, which went into effect the following day.

At his home in Manshiet al-Bakry, Nasser finally understood the true scale of the disaster. The world had changed since 1956, when he had pulled a political victory out of a military defeat before the astonished eyes of Britain, France and Israel. In 1956 he had watched newsreels of anti-war protestors in London, urging Egypt to stand firm and condemning Eden's imperial pretensions. In 1967 Egypt's defiance only seemed to turn sympathy towards Israel. In the words of one contemporary observer: 'the Israelis, with a better grasp of the realities of Western war, restrained their words and when they struck, struck hard, killed thousands and much of the West cheered as if it were watching a football match'.[168] The Soviet Union had not moved to help Egypt, and Nasser believed that the US was actively supporting Israel.

However, the cruellest blow of the war was its exposure of the hollowness of the army regime. For fifteen years, the Egyptian army had spoken in the name of the nation. Since 1952, when the army finally stepped into the battle for national liberation, the young officers had believed that they alone could lead Egypt. Nasser's success in playing Great Power politics had brought Egypt the latest Soviet equipment, but the men in command seemed to have failed the test of war. Stories circulated about chaos in the commander-in-chief's office. The atmosphere at headquarters was 'like a terrifying nightmare'.[169] Amer had ordered an immediate withdrawal from Sinai on 6 June, but Nasser overruled him, and commanded Egyptian forces to stand and fight at the passes in the mountains. Conflicting orders and mounting panic turned the military disaster into a catastrophe as Egyptian units collided with each other and their commanding officers fled.

On the evening of 9 June, Nasser gave his first broadcast since the start of the war. In a speech to the National Assembly, he took full responsibility for the *grave setback* of the previous few days. He told his listeners that despite the efforts of her allies in the Arab world, Egypt had suffered a terrible defeat. *I am ready to take complete responsibility. I have taken a decision in which I want you all to help me. I have decided to give up completely and finally every official post and political role and return to the ranks of the masses and do my duty with them like every other citizen. The forces of colonialism believe that Gamal Abd-al-Nasser is their enemy. I want to make it clear to them that their enemy is the entire Arab nation, not merely Gamal Abd-al-Nasser. ... In doing this I am not liquidating the revolution; the revolution is not the monopoly of any single generation of revolutionaries ... This is an hour for action; not an hour for sorrow.*[170]

Nearly two years younger than Nasser, Abd-al-Hakim Amer (1919 – 1967) graduated from the Military Academy in 1939. He became friends with Nasser when they were posted together to Khartoum in the early 1940s. He was one of the founding members of the Free Officers and played an important role during the July revolution. His appointment as Commander-in-Chief of Egypt's armed forces in 1953 was widely seen as Nasser's first blow in the battle for power with Naguib.

Abd-al-Hakim Amer was the only person who knew of Nasser's intentions that night. He had not even told the Vice-President, Zakaria Mohi-al-Din, who he named as his successor in his resignation speech.[171] Within hours thousands of people were taking to the streets across Egypt to demand that Nasser stay. 'In the twilight and the semi blacked-out streets, hundreds of thousands, some of the men still in pyjamas and the women in nightgowns, came out of their houses weeping and

Israeli soldier on the East bank of the Suez Canal, 1967

shouting, "Nasser, Nasser, don't leave us, we need you". The noise was like a rising storm.'[172] Among the cries for Nasser to stay were other slogans, messages to the watching superpowers. 'The streets of Cairo were flooded with more than two and half million; the whole population of Tantah, the centre of the Delta, was marching on the capital ... from every city, town and village, from Alexandria to Aswan, from the Western Desert to Suez, a whole nation marched. And its slogans could not be misunderstood: "No imperialism, no dollar!"; "No leader but Gamal!"'.[173]

The following day, Nasser withdrew his resignation. To many Western observers, his sudden change of heart could only mean that the whole episode was a repeat of the stage-managed protests of 1954. Others who watched his haggard performance on 9 June thought differently: 'Egyptians did not judge Nasser simply by his success or failure as a military leader ... He was rather the man who had overthrown the King, ended the British occupation, given Egypt full control of the Suez Canal, begun to build the High Dam, carried through the land reform and tried to control rents, built more factories and schools, brought clean water and electricity to many more villages, begun social insurance for workers and within limits given many more Egyptians a say in the running of their own affairs.'[174] As in 1956, many of Nassers' left-wing opponents now rallied behind him. The anti-imperialist slogans on the demonstrations were also a warning to Nasser's designated successor, Zakaria Mohi-al-Din, seen by many in Egypt as the most pro-American member of the government.

The reversal of Nasser's fortune was confirmed at a summit meeting in the Sudanese capital Khartoum, where hundreds of thousands lined the streets to cheer for him, prompting a sardonic headline on the front cover of Newsweek: 'Hail the conquered'.

'The system is eating itself'

Nasser had been confirmed in power by a spontaneous popular upsurge of support, but most Egyptians were less inclined to forgive the performance of his brother officers. The army had failed to defend the country in its hour of need, despite the boasts of its leaders. The gap between reality and the bombast from Voice of the Arabs radio was painfully large.

For many the root of the problem lay in the increasing dislocation of the 'officer class' from the rest of the population. Propelled into the front rank of the political leadership by their coup in 1952, many of the young officers and their followers saw the state as little more than a mechanism for self-enrichment and self-aggrandizement – or so it seemed to many ordinary Egyptians. Unlike Nasser, who avoided displays of wealth, some of his fellow officers were known for their taste for the high-life. This was not simply a problem of individual decadence, it was the flip-side of the creation of a new ruling class; the officers were embedded at the highest levels of the government and the command economy. Military defeat provided the catalyst for the expression of deeper social discontent. After a long silence, Nasser acknowledged the problems in a speech on 23 July, marking the fifteenth anniversary of the revolution. He promised to look inwards, towards solving Egypt's economic and social problems and in a reference to public fury at the military leadership, he admitted: *The people have been demanding a limit to the privilege which some had acquired without good reason, and I am with the people on this. We, the people, are building our socialist society. This society is not for a privileged class, indeed it is in its very nature to oppose class distinction.*[175]

Nasser faced an immediate challenge, however, from the leadership of the army. As he prepared to resign, he told his commander-in-chief, Abd-al-Hakim Amer, to do the same. After he withdrew his resignation he sacked Amer and fifty senior commanders on 11 June. Nasser was confronted at his home by a group of young officers calling on him to reinstate Amer. He persuaded the officers to leave with a promise that he would set up a committee to look into their grievances, but took to sleeping with a pistol under his pillow.

Amer was named as one of seven vice-presidents, but was arrested and accused of plotting a coup aimed at halting the investigation into the army's collapse in June. He was said to have committed suicide by swallowing poison before he could be brought to court.[176] Several of his colleagues, including the former Minister of War, Shams-al-Din Badran, received long prison sentences in a series of 'treason trials' in 1968.

Amer had been one of Nasser's closest colleagues and friends for nearly thirty years. He was one of the few who had retained Nasser's trust as he became increasingly isolated from the rest of the Free Officers. They were even related by marriage, and Abd-al-Hakim, one of Nasser's sons, bore Amer's name. Yet at the same time the logic of Nasser's move against what he called *the new class*[177] meant that Amer had to be broken, even in death. Newspapers were fed lurid 'revelations' about Amer's womanising and drug-taking. Nasser told colleagues on the executive of the Arab Socialist Union that Amer's attempted coup threatened the fabric of the state. *All these activities have been carried out by the people closest to me and by the command structures closest to the regime, what sort of actions might not be perpetrated by others? ... These days it is being said throughout the country that we are eating each other and that the system is eating itself.*[178] In this way Nasser's sense of 'metaphysical union' with the Egyptian body politic emerged as a psychologically destructive force. His struggle against 'the new class' developed 'in him and outside him like an internal disease, growing day by day until it defeated him without shedding a drop of blood.'[179]

He was not merely facing pressure from his disaffected generals. The defeat widened divisions within the Egyptian leadership as those who wanted Nasser's experiment in state socialism to end, pinned their hopes on a rapprochement with the USA. Just a month after the war, Nasser told Soviet President Podgorny that he was under pressure from inside the regime. *There is a faction in this country ... that holds me personally responsible for everything that happened because I undermined the relationship with America*[180]

Yet while sections of Egypt's elite swung further towards the USA, Nasser also faced criticism from ordinary Egyptians for failing to curb the power of the officer class. The *Times* correspondent in Cairo reported that after the defeat 'soldiers were insulted in the Cairo streets so frequently that they were instructed not to go about town in uniform except when compelled to do so by duty.'[181] The mood of the country was clear when the verdicts were announced in the 'treason trials'. In February 1968 the working- class district of Helwan on the outskirts of Cairo was convulsed by massive demonstrations, which quickly spread to university campuses in Cairo and Alexandria. [182] Protestors besieged the National Assembly and the offices of Muhammad Hassanein Heikal's newspaper, *Al-Ahram*, chanting 'No leniency for the traitors' and 'No socialism without freedom'. In November four students were killed in a clash with police in Mansoura, and around 5,000 students and workers took to the streets of Alexandria. For the first time slogans calling on Nasser to resign were heard. [183]

Friends and enemies

At this time of crisis, Nasser's instinct was to turn back to his old colleagues in the Free Officers' Command Council, but those bonds had been finally shattered by Amer's death. In July 1968 he wrote to Abd-al-Latif al-Bughdadi, who had resigned from government back in 1962 in protest at Nasser's move towards the USSR, asking him to return. Bughdadi replied that he would rather be Nasser's friend than his prime minister and experience had taught him that he could not be both. [184] In private he confided in his diaries that he accepted Amer's family's claim that the Field Marshal had been murdered by the government. [185] In reality, the independent-minded among Nasser's colleagues had long been alienated by his decision to distance himself from them as he became more and more wrapped up in his public persona: 'Al-Ra'is'. Nasser's adoption of his new identity, sat uneasily with his strong sense of personal morality. As Said Aburish puts it, 'his were the deeds of a divided person, as always someone whose dictatorial behaviour was in direct conflict with his very genuine commitment to the honour and dignity of the common man.' [186]

At times he tried to make amends for the damage that the exercise of his power caused to personal relationships. Ihsan Abd-al-Quddus was the owner of the satirical magazine, *Rose el-Youssef* when he first met Nasser before the revolution. In an interview with *Al-Ahram* many years later he recalled vividly the taciturn, reserved officer, whom he called by his nickname, 'Jimmy'. In 1954 Abd-al-Quddus was arrested and spent three months in jail for writing an article calling on Nasser to leave the army and form a normal political party. On his return home he picked up the phone to hear Nasser's voice at the other end: *Have you learned your lesson, Ihsan?* At dinner a few nights later, Nasser was more conciliatory. *'It's true that I had you put in prison without having read that article you wrote. I had you arrested on the basis of what I was told about the article. It seems, Ihsan, that I was misinformed.* He fell silent. When I did not respond, he continued, *Anyway, when I did read the article, I realised you were speaking your mind, as you always do.'* Several years later, Abd-al-Quddus was jailed again, but he had only been in detention for a few hours when Nasser called the prison and asked to speak to him. *What can I say, Ihsan? I never ordered your arrest or anything like that. Since you're in the military prison, I have Abd-al-Hakim next to me and he's going to apologise on behalf of the whole army.*[187]

As the history of the Free Officers shows, Nasser's personal dictatorship was still a long way from the blood-soaked follies of Saddam Hussein's Iraq. Unlike the Ba'athist strongman's colleagues, most of the members of the original Command Council outlived Nasser. Once he considered a colleague was no longer a political threat, Nasser was generally kinder than most dictators. Outside the circle of the Free Officers, it was a different matter as Nasser's implacable hatred of the Muslim Brotherhood and the persecution of the Communists demonstrates.

The exception to the rule, was of course Amer. While Nasser became estranged from many of his former colleagues, most of his biographers agree that his relationship with Amer was the one fatal occasion when loyalty and friendship overrode his common sense. Time and again Nasser relied on Amer, entrusting him with the command of the army, appointing him his deputy in Syria during the years of union, with disastrous results. Amer's promotion to Commander-in-Chief, a strictly political manoeuvre designed to squeeze Muhammad Naguib out of power in 1953, was the only accelerated military promotion among the Free Officers. Nasser himself changed out of his fatigues and put on a civilian suit after the first few years in power. By the early 1960s Nasser and Amer's relationship had begun to sour, but it was too late. Amer was too well-entrenched in the army to be removed without risking open warfare at the heart of the regime.

Negotiations with the Soviets

Nasser announced a series of political reforms, hoping to breathe life into the Arab Socialist Union, which had been set up to replace the National Union as the party of the state, although he also denounced the protests as the work of Israeli agents. Elections took place for a new ASU executive and Nasser considered legalising other parties. The press laws were relaxed, and the government took some small steps towards a more liberal economy. At the same time, further loans were received from the USSR and hundreds of Soviet technicians arrived to help rebuild Egypt's shattered armed forces.

The end of the war in June 1967 had not brought real peace – Sinai was under Israeli occupation. Nasser could do little but build his forces and maintain a war of attrition with Israeli forces on the East Bank of the Canal. His priority was to rearm as quickly as possible. Soviet Premier Podgorny visited Cairo and Nasser argued for an increase in Russian aid to repair the damage done by the Israeli attack. His bargaining position was weak, and he knew it, but he still tried to stave off Soviet pressure to open a military base on Egyptian soil. As Muhammad Hassanein Heikal puts it 'he was trying to make the Russians see Egypt's defeat as their defeat, and to increase their aid to

Nasser in Moscow, 1969

Egypt, even to the extent of taking over, temporarily at least, Egypt's air defences, but at the same time was telling them 'no base; no red flag".[188]

During talks with Brezhnev in Moscow he threatened to resign, to the consternation of the Soviet leaders. '"Comrade Nasser, don't talk like this. You are the leader..." Nasser interrupted: *I am a leader who is bombed everyday in his own country, whose army is exposed and whose people are naked. I have the courage to tell our people the unfortunate truth – that whether they like it or not, the Americans are masters of the world. I am not going to be the one who surrenders to the Americans. Someone else will come in my place who will have to do it.*'[189]

Nasser's trips to Moscow also gave him the opportunity to consult Soviet doctors about his health. Abd-al-Magid Farid, Secretary at the presidency, describes how the defeat of 1967 had taken a physical toll. 'The six days of war had immediately added ten years to his life. Already suffering from diabetes, he was now having to cope with severe leg pains that left him unable to stand for long. He was disinclined to talk, and seemed deeply troubled. All of us who were close to him felt that because of this anger, grief and pain, the heart had gone out of him.' [190]

In public he said little about his worries. A heart attack in September 1969 was passed off as influenza. Muhammad Hasanein Heikal described seeing him in his bedroom shortly afterwards. Still pale and weak from the shock, Nasser complained that the Soviet specialists had not only banned him from using the phone, they also expected him to give up smoking. After three days' frustration, he was back at his desk.[191]

He did finally seek some help to ease the burden of work, however. His eldest daughter, Hoda, now herself a mother to Nasser's granddaughter, became his secretary and nurse around this time. Despite the intellectual fulfilment that their work together brought her, Hoda later recalled her father at this period as a driven man, 'physically ill and emotionally strained.'[192]

The rise of the guerrillas

Outside Egypt, others seemed to have found a different strategy to confront Israel. Disillusioned by the failure of the radical nationalist states, and particularly by the humbling of Nasser, young Palestinians were flocking to join the guerrilla movements. While the Arab leaders seemed paralysed by the restrictions of international diplomacy, a new generation of activists was taking the fight direct to the enemy. In March 1968, Yasser Arafat's Fatah movement caught the attention of the world, when the Israelis sustained heavy losses attacking the village of Karameh in the West Bank. Although the guerrillas' base was surrounded, they fought fiercely, rescuing, some said, the honour of the Arabs after the humiliation of the Six Day War. The name of Karameh – 'dignity' in Arabic – eased some of the painful memories of 1967.

Nasser's attitude to the guerrillas was ambivalent. He was initially supportive and allowed Fatah's guerrillas to train in Egypt. The movement set up a radio station in Cairo. At a secret meeting with Yasser Arafat, Salah Khalaf and Farouq Qaddumi, Nasser explained that although Egypt had accepted UN Resolution 242, and thus implicitly Israel's right to exist, the Palestinians should not be bound by the same considerations. *You have every right not to accept it ... there is no reason why you should not publicly oppose the resolution because it is not designed for you. But why not be our Stern {Gang}? Why not be our {Menachem} Begin? You must be our irresponsible arm. On this basis we will give you all the help we can.*[193]

However, he feared a movement which was not under his control, and which could not be trusted to hold back its members at times when delicate diplomacy was needed. The rise of the guerrillas was a challenge to Nasser's vision of Arab nationalism. For the leaders of Fatah, the time had passed when Palestinians should defer to Egypt and Nasser as the 'leader' of the Arab world. Unlike the previous leaders of the Palestinian movement, such as Ahmad al-Shuqairi, who had been hand-picked by the Egyptian government, Yasser Arafat did not shrink from criticism, when in July 1970 Nasser announced his acceptance of a plan sponsored by US Secretary of State William Rogers, to bring peace between Israel and her Arab neighbours on the basis of UN resolution 242.

King Hussein of Jordan followed Egypt's lead, and Israel agreed to the 'Rogers Plan' in August. For Nasser, the most important result of the peace proposals was the implementation of a ceasefire along the Suez Canal, suspending the punishing war of attrition with Israeli forces. To the Palestinians it appeared that Egypt was about to conclude a separate peace with Israel and abandon them to fight alone.

By September 1970 Fatah had established itself as the leading Palestinian movement. Yasser Arafat had been elected leader of the Palestine Liberation Organisation in 1969. At the same time, Fatah had built a substantial base in the Palestinian refugee camps of Amman. The bulk of Jordan's population is Palestinian, but the King and most of the ruling elite are not. Hundreds of thousands of new refugees had crowded into Amman after fleeing their homes as the Israelis invaded the West Bank in 1967. The guerrilla movements won many supporters in the years after 1967 and Fatah's armed forces soon controlled large parts of the city.

Fatah was not without its rivals – radical nationalist and left-wing groups such as the Popular Front for the Liberation of Palestine (PFLP), founded by George Habash. Although Fatah was critical of the Arab governments, Yasser Arafat attempted to tread a narrow path between antagonism and alliance. Fatah's focus was also primarily on the struggle to liberate Palestinian soil from Israeli occupation – so the guerrillas chose targets inside Israel or in the occupied territories. The PFLP saw the 'liberation struggle' as part of a wider movement linking the fight against imperialism across the globe.

Black September

In September 1970 PFLP members attempted the simultaneous hijacking of four commercial airliners. Three groups of hijackers were successful, although the fourth failed. One hijacker on board an El-Al flight to Heathrow was killed, and the other, 24-year old Leila Khaled, was captured. Three of the planes were flown to an airstrip in the desert near Amman and blown up by the hijackers, after the passengers had been evacuated. Negotiations then began for the release of the passengers, whom the hijackers wanted to exchange for Leila Khaled and several other Palestinians imprisoned in Israel and Europe.

Nasser was asked by the US to intervene in the negotiations, and was able to use his influence to help the peaceful settlement of the hijackings. Leila Khaled was flown to Beirut by the RAF and the hostages were released. A few days later, King Hussein ordered the regular Jordanian army to move against the Palestinian guerrillas. Fighting engulfed large parts of Amman, and although the guerrillas were outnumbered they put up a stubborn defence. Jordan seemed in danger of collapsing as the civil war spread. US President Nixon's National Security Advisor, Henry Kissinger, had already prepared two contingency plans: in one scenario the Israelis would have the task of reacting to moves by Syria and Iraq to help the guerrillas, while US forces evacuated American civilians from Jordan. Kissinger later recorded that he felt that the US decision to put troops on alert in Europe and the Mediterranean had played an important role in convincing King Hussein to move against the Palestinians.[194] US backing for King Hussein also had its effect on the rest of the Arab world: Syria was the only country to answer the Palestinians' desperate call for aid, but now Soviet pressure stopped the advance of Syrian tanks into Jordan.

At a hastily-convened summit meeting in the Nile Hilton in Cairo Nasser attempted to broker a ceasefire. Muhammad Hassanein Heikal, at that time Minister of National Guidance and editor of the

Arab Summit frustrations: Nile Hilton, 1970

daily *Al-Ahram*, remembered later the tension as the heads of state waited for Nasser to arrive. King Hussein and Yasser Arafat, who were both armed with pistols, glowered at each other from opposite corners of the room. Heikal half-jokingly suggested to King Faisal of Saudi Arabia that a 'disarmament operation' would be needed before the summit could begin. 'Only Nasser can do that' replied Faisal.[195] After hours of tense negotiations Arafat and Hussein agreed to a ceasefire; although the guerrillas would have to leave Amman, the killing would stop, at least for the time being.

The meeting exposed once again the deep divisions between the Arab leaders. At the summit, Mu'ammar al-Gadaffy, who had seized power in Libya the year before, put forward a resolution calling for a joint Arab invasion of Jordan to defeat King Hussein, who he said was 'a madman'. Not for the first time, Nasser found himself trying to hold back both the radical nationalists who saw King Hussein as a proxy for US imperialism, and the pro-Western leaders who saw the guerrillas as a threat to regional stability. Back in August, before the PFLP hijackings, he warned King Hussein against taking advantage of the Rogers Plan to rid himself of the guerrillas. *No doubt you have the strength to crush them, but to do this you will have to slaughter 20,000 people and your kingdom will be a kingdom of ghosts.* [196]

An agreement was signed and released and one by one the rulers departed. Nasser saw them off at the airport, although he was already beginning to feel sharp pains in his chest. Photographs taken as he bade farewell to the Emir of Qatar show him smiling, but his fist hung clenched at his side. He returned home to Manshiet al-Bakry, sweating and ill. Three hours later he was dead. When Egyptians turned on the radio that evening, it was Anwar Sadat's voice that they heard, pledging to continue Nasser's policies as Egypt's new President.

Nasser's legacy

Asked by a British journalist what he thought was his greatest achievement, Nasser replied that it was the original coup in 1952. For him, the revolution of 1952 was the foundation on which his efforts to create new opportunities for ordinary Egyptians were based. He gave an example: *My driver's son is able to go to university while my daughter could not get in because she had not high enough marks. So I had to send my daughter to the American University here and pay £100 a year for her, while my driver's son goes to Cairo University for free. Some think that the nationalisation of the Suez Canal Company or the 1961 nationalisations were the main achievements but they were only steps towards the aim of equality of opportunity.*[197]

In this respect, Nasser's practical legacy has proved less resilient than his status as an icon of Arab pride. Over the three decades since his death, many of his policies have been reversed. Nasserist parties now find themselves in opposition to Nasser's heirs at the helm of the Egyptian state.

'Hero of the crossing, where is our breakfast?'[198]

Three days after his death, Nasser's coffin was taken through Cairo to be buried. Statesmen had to be whisked away from the raw grief of the crowds, fearing they would be trampled. The banks of the Nile filled with weeping, chanting mourners. As they had done three years before after the defeat of 1967, millions poured into the streets, this time to pay their last respects. The opening lines of Nizar Qabbani's poem, 'Gamal Abd-al-Nasser' published the following year, sum up the mood of time: 'Last of the prophets, we killed you'. [199] Nasser's funeral seemed to mark a watershed in Egyptian political culture. Neither of Nasser's successors managed to fill the streets in the same way. At the funeral of Anwar Sadat, assassinated by Islamic Jihad in October 1981, world leaders walked through near-empty streets behind the President's coffin.

'Last of the prophets, we killed you.'

For many on the Egyptian left, Sadat emerges as the authentic villain of the drama of the 1970s. He railed against the 'stupid kind of socialism'[200] of the 1960s, opened the Egyptian economy to foreign investment, and concluded peace with Israel, making Egypt a pariah in the Arab world.

Muhammad Hassanein Heikal thought that Egypt had returned to the 19th century: 'not since the days of Khedive Ismail had Egypt been the scene of looting on such a massive and organized scale as it was during the last years of President Sadat.'[201]

Many ordinary Egyptians seemed to agree: during the huge protests which forced Sadat to reverse his policy of lifting subsidies on basic foods in 1977, crowds mocked their sharp-suited President and his glamorous wife. 'Down with Sadat's palaces!' 'Jehan, Jehan, the people are hungry'. 'Nasser always said: "take care of the workers".'[202]

Yet, how much of Sadat's road to economic liberalisation and accommodation with the West would Nasser have travelled, had he lived? In the changed economic climate of the 1970s he would have found it hard to resist the pressure to move away from state-led development towards the free market. For Ghali Shoukri, Nasser's revolution and Sadat's 'counter-revolution' were two sides of the same coin. 'The Egyptian writer Abbas Mahmud al-Aqqad often said: "God only knows if Lucifer's revolt was revolution or counter-revolution" . . . Nasser's putsch would have suggested this reply to him: Lucifer's revolt is a revolution and counter-revolution at the same time.'[203] Sadat was as much part of the

Born into a peasant family in a Delta village, Anwar Sadat (1918 – 1981) joined the Military Academy at the same time as Nasser. Sadat was initially far more active in politics than Nasser. Imprisoned by the British during World War Two for treason, he made a name for himself as a dare-devil conspirator, but was also discharged from the army and spent much of the 1940s as a civilian. Sadat had just rejoined the military at the time the Free Officers were formed.

Under Nasser he spent a long period as Speaker of the National Assembly, and was appointed Vice-President for the first time in 1964. He succeeded Nasser as President in 1970 after Nasser's sudden death from a heart attack.

'officer class' as Nasser. The people who benefited from his policy of liberalisation, *infitah* in Arabic, were those linked to the existing structures of power, not an external capitalist class. The crisis of the command economy in the mid 1960s had already created the conditions for a revival of the private sector before Nasser's death.

Jehan and Anwar Sadat

In foreign policy, Sadat appeared at first to be continuing Nasser's legacy. He used the Rogers Plan to create a breathing space in which to rearm and rebuild Egypt's armed forces. Then in 1973 Egypt and Syria launched simultaneous attacks on Israel from the Golan Heights and across the Suez Canal. This time it was the Israeli army's turn to be taken unawares, and Egyptian forces managed to push the Israeli forces back over the Canal. Although the Israeli army rallied and counter-attacked, the initial success of the attack was felt by many in the Arab world to have wiped out some of the shame of 1967.

Within a few years, however, Sadat was deep in peace negotiations with Israel, even visiting Jerusalem to speak to the Knesset in 1977. From being the leader of the Arab world, Egypt became overnight a pariah, although initially Sadat faced little overt opposition at home over his new policy. In 1979 he signed a peace treaty with Israel at Camp David, which regained Sinai for Egypt but led to the country's expulsion from the Arab League and Egypt's diplomatic isolation. In 1981, as he was reviewing the troops on the anniversary of the 1973 war with Israel, Sadat was assassinated by militants from Islamic Jihad, an underground Islamist organisation.

Return of consciousness

While protestors still invoked Nasser's name against his successors, for some Egyptians the 1970s marked the start of a reappraisal of his legacy. Tawfiq al-Hakim was one of those who led the way in 1974, publishing an extended essay entitled *Return of Consciousness*, in which he criticised Nasser for acting as an 'idol'. Egypt had become accustomed to one-man rule, he said, and this was why Nasser had the power to 'paralyse the mind so that the people see nothing except what he sees and be permitted no view contrary to his view.'[204] Intoxicated by Nasser's rhetoric, Egyptians failed to see that he was leading the country to defeat after defeat. 'When he delivered a powerful speech and said about a strong country which had the atomic bomb that *if they don't like our conduct, let them drink from the sea* we were filled with pride.'[205] It was only the disaster of June 1967 which brought Al-Hakim to his senses at last. Al-Hakim's criticism of Nasser reversed his earlier enthusiasm for the Free Officers' 'blessed movement', which he had hailed in his writings of the 1950s. In the world of the 1970s, the confident nationalism of an earlier age now seemed not just out-of-place, but reckless.

Egypt since Sadat

Hosni Mubarak, Sadat's successor, continued his reforms at a slower pace. He battled with radical Islamist groups, sending troops to fight armed militants in the Nile valley. Thousands were arrested and hundreds of suspects killed in an increasingly violent campaign, after the Islamists attacked foreign tourists. Growing economic problems brought more loans from the IMF and World Bank. During the 1990s this policy began to pick up speed, as increasing numbers of state enterprises were privatised.

The privatisation programme was only part of a wider shift in policy, aimed at undoing key aspects of Nasser's economic legacy. Thousands of workers were laid off, and new laws brought in, ending some of the protection enjoyed by employees since the 1950s. In 1997 the land reform of 1952 was rescinded, removing the upper limit on landownership. Large-scale protests by tenant farmers, share-croppers and rural labourers failed to deter the government. Rents on housing were also liberalised. By the beginning of the new century, privatisation had been extended to parts of the education system, and a further change in the labour laws allowed companies to hire and fire at will. The Nasserist welfare state was allowed to decay: throughout the 1980s and 1990s spending on health and education stagnated or fell, despite Egypt's soaring population.

In foreign policy Mubarak also built on Sadat's legacy. He gradually brought Egypt out of diplomatic isolation in the Arab world, while retaining Sadat's strong links with the USA. Sadat's peace deal with Israel brought Egypt closer to the US than ever before in its history. The end of the Cold War and the collapse of the Soviet Union seemed to leave Egypt's neighbours with little choice: make peace with the one remaining superpower or suffer the same fate as Iraq, defeated and besieged after invading Kuwait in August 1990. Egypt played an important role in the peace negotiations between the PLO and Israel, which led to the setting up of the Palestinian Authority in 1994. However, the disintegration of the peace process in the late 1990s and the growing popular support for the Palestinians has put the Egyptian government's pro-Western orientation under pressure.

Nasserism without Nasser?

While in power, much of Nasser's appeal was based on his image as a charismatic leader, who could rise above social class and political faction to represent the whole nation. Even when his subordinates were criticised for corruption or incompetence, Nasser himself often escaped condemnation.

The effect of Nasser's popular image is double-edged. On the one hand it nourishes a nostalgia for Nasser's era: in 1996 cinema audiences flocked to see a film of Nasser's exploits during the Suez Crisis. At the Egyptian State Book Organisation they may look at you blankly if you ask for *Philosophy of the Revolution*, but glossy photo albums of Nasser's life still sell well in the bookshops in Cairo. On the other hand, Nasser's popularity did not translate into a party that could sustain itself independently of the Egyptian state. Nasser's role as a figurehead for the Arab revolution only developed after he took control of the government. It was by using the machinery of the state – in particular the Ministry of the Interior and the army – that he defeated his opponents inside and outside the government in March 1954.

Today's Nasserists would also face great obstacles if they did reverse the tide of history and regain state power. Changes in the world economy over the past three decades have left little space for the kind of autonomous development Nasser hoped was possible in the 1960s. Many of the most profitable parts of the Egyptian economy have been sold to foreign multinationals. The Soviet Union vanished long ago, leaving most leaders of 'developing countries' little choice but to seek political and economic patronage from the USA. In the Middle East, Israel is more powerful and better armed than in 1967, and the prospects for peace with the Palestinians are as distant as ever. Meanwhile, Arab summits are still as bad-tempered as they were in 1970, and the prospects for unity seem bleak.

Secular nationalists in the Middle East today also face competition from powerful rival ideologies, in particular the Islamist movement which began to revive during the 1970s. As Arab leaders have retreated from confrontation with the West, Islamists have often led protests against 'American imperialism' and peace with Israel. The decay of the welfare state has also created new spaces for Islamic activism. Nasser's old foes, the Muslim Brotherhood, are the largest opposition movement in Egypt, and maintain their political base partly by providing clinics, schools and basic services to thousands of Egypt's poor.

Even while Nasser was alive, Islamist activists were laying the intellectual foundations for this revival. The Islamist intellectual Sayyid Qutb, who was hanged by Nasser in 1966, wrote that Egyptian society had reverted to a state of pre-Islamic barbarism, or *jahiliyya*. Although the mainstream of the Brotherhood rejected it, his analysis later inspired radical Islamists to take up arms against Anwar Sadat.

Despite this, much of what Nasser seemed to stand for in the 1950s and 1960s remains potent for a new generation. Years of structural adjustment have not brought prosperity for most Egyptians. The government's decades-old alliance with the US has not succeeded in bringing peace to the Middle East nor secured justice for the Palestinians. Nearly fifty years after the overthrow of the Iraqi monarchy, foreign troops returned to occupy a key Arab state. For many in the Arab world, the presence of US and British forces on Arab soil is simply a return to the old-fashioned colonialism.

Nasser, surrounded by his three sons

Just as these things angered Nasser and his friends, so they continue to enrage new generations of activists. In a sense, today's protestors have much in common with the activists of the forties. They have found little echo among the established political parties in Egypt, which have been largely absent from the streets. British colonialism has been replaced by American imperialism as the target for their protests. And some of the biggest demonstrations have turned their anger from foreign to domestic policy, as chants go up against rising prices and corruption.

Between 2000 and 2003 Egypt was shaken by some of the largest protests since the 1970s. Thousands of students demonstrated in support of the Palestinians in September 2000. Tens of thousands marched again in April 2002, after Israeli tanks laid siege to Yasser Arafat's headquarters in Ramallah. Around thirty thousand people defied the police to demonstrate in Tahrir Square in the centre of Cairo in March 2003 as US and British forces invaded Iraq. Nasser's picture has also made a sudden reappearance, carried aloft by protestors not only in Cairo, but also in Beirut and Amman.

Within the Egyptian state, much of Nasser's legacy has been erased. In the streets, however, the spirit of the movement which catapulted him into power may be still alive.

Notes

1 Gamal Abd-al-Nasser, *The Philosophy of the Revolution*, (Dar al-Sha'ab, Cairo: n.d, 9th edition), pp 36-7, in Arabic

2 Quoted in Rosa Luxemburg, *The Accumulation of Capital* (Monthly Review Press, New York:1968) p 437

3 *The Economist,* 17 June 1882, p735

4 P. J. Vatikiotis, *A History of Modern Egypt* (Weidenfeld and Nicolson, London:1991), p 178

5 Salama Musa, quoted in E. Davies, *Challenging Colonialism: Bank Misr and Egyptian industrialization 1920–1941* (Princeton University Press, Princeton, NJ: 1983), p 45

6 Robert Stephens, *Nasser* (Penguin, London:1971) p 31-2

7 Stephens, *Nasser*, p 28

8 Quoted in Paul Starkey, *From the Ivory Tower: A critical study of Tawfiq al-Hakim* (Ithaca press, Reading: 1987), p 90

9 Quoted in Starkey, *From the Ivory Tower*, p 125

10 Published in English translation as *The Maze of Justice* (Saqi Books, London: 1989)

11 Al-Hakim, *The Maze of Justice*, p 112

12 Stephens, *Nasser*, p 35

13 Joel Beinin and Lockman, *Workers on the Nile* (Princeton University Press, Princeton, NJ: 1988), p218

14 Stephens, *Nasser*, p 56

15 Khaled Mohi-al-Din, *Memories of a Revolution* (American University in Cairo Press, Cairo: 1995) p 17

16 Communist Party Archives, *National Museum of Labour History*, Manchester, CP/CENT/INT/56/04

17 Anwar Sadat, *Revolt on the Nile*,1957 quoted in Jean Lacouture, *Nasser* (Secker and Warburg, London: 1973), p 44

18 Stephens, *Nasser*, p 53

19 Mohi-al-Din, *Memories*, p 39-40

20 P.J. Vatikiotis, *A History of Modern Egypt* (Weidenfeld and Nicolson, London:1991), p 354

21 Mohi-al-Din, *Memories*, p 23

22 Mohi-al-Din, *Memories*, p 25

23 Gilles Perrault, *A Man Apart: a Life of Henri Curiel* (Zed Books, London: 1987), p 120

24 *Egyptian Gazette*, Alexandria, 6 and 7 April 1948

25 Ahmad Hamroush, interview with the author, Cairo, 8 September 1996

26 Muhammad Naguib, *Egypt's Destiny* (Victor Gollancz, London:1955), p 17

27 Stephens, *Nasser*, p 78

28 Gamal Abd-al-Nasser,'Speech in Alexandria, 18 April 1953', from Gamal
    Abd-al-Nasser, *Speeches and briefings by Gamal Abd-al-Nasser 1952-59*, Cairo,
    Sharikat al-Alanat al-Sharqiyya, 1959, in Arabic p 56
29 Naguib, *Egypt's Destiny*, p 21
30 Stephens, *Nasser*, p 79
31 Mohi-al-Din, *Memories*, p 45
32 Ghali Shoukri, *Egypt: portrait of a president – Sadat's road to Jerusalem* (Zed
    Books, London: 1981), p 38
33 Naguib, *Egypt's Destiny*, p 29
34 Jean and Simonne Lacouture, *Egypt in Transition* (Methuen, London:
    1958), p 108
35 Lacoutures, *Egypt*, p 109
36 Nasser, *Philosophy*, p 41-43
37 Mohi-al-Din, *Memories*, p 100
38 Anwar Sadat, *In search of identity – an autobiography* (Harper and Row, New
    York: 1977), p 107
39 Rifaat al-Sa'id, interview with the author, Cairo, 12 September 1996
40 Naguib, *Egypt's Destiny*, p 132
41 Naguib, *Egypt's Destiny*, p 140
42 Sadat, *In search*, p 120
43 Mohi-al-Din, *Memories*, p 115
44 Mohi-al-Din, *Memories*, p 120
45 Stephens, *Nasser*, p 112
46 Stephens, *Nasser*, p 113
47 Gamal Abd-al-Nasser, 'Speech to transport workers', 29 April 1954, trans-
    lated from audio recording in Arabic on the Nasser Foundation   web
    site, www.nasser.org
48 Fathallah Mahrus, interview with the author, Cairo, 15 December 2003
49 Beinin and Lockman, *Workers*, p 427
50 'Summary of Articles from *Al-Malayin*, 10 September 1952', Communist
    Party Archives, National Museum of Labour History, Manchester,
    CP/CENT/INT/56/04
51 Fathallah Mahrus, interview with the author, Cairo, 15 December 2003
52 Ahmad Hamroush, interview with the author, Cairo, 8 September 1996
53 Makram 'Ubayd, quoted in Marius Deeb, 'Large Landowners and
    Social Transformation in Egypt 1940-52,' in Tarif Khalidi (ed), *Land Tenure
    and Social Transformation in the Middle East* (American University   in
    Beirut Press, Beirut: 1984), p 433
54 Doreen Warriner, *Land Reform and Development in the Middle East* (Oxford
    University Press, London:1962), p 13
55 Richard P. Mitchell, *The Society of the Muslim Brothers* (Oxford University
    Press, London:1969, p105
56 Mitchell, *The Society*, p106
57 Naguib, *Egypt's Destiny*, picture, centre pages
58 *The Times*, London, 18 November 1952
59 Jean Lacouture, *The Demigods: charismatic leadership in the Third World*, (Alfred
    A. Knopf, New York: 1970), p 92
60 Nasser, *Philosophy*, p 22
61 Gamal Abd-al-Nasser, 'Speech in Shubin al-Kum', 23 February 1953,
    in Gamal Abd-al-Nasser, *Speeches and briefings by Gamal Abd-al-Nasser 1952-
    59* (Sharikat al-Alanat al-Sharqiyya, Cairo: 1959), in Arabic, p 12
62 In *The Philosophy of the Revolution,* Nasser explains the slogan as a reaction
    to the confusion of the early days in power. Nasser, *Philosophy*, p 23

63 Lacouture, *The Demigods*, p100
64 Nasser, *Philosophy*, p 23
65 Lacouture, *The Demigods*, p 94
66 Naguib, *Egypt's Destiny*, p 216
67 Naguib, *Egypt's Destiny*, p 214
68 Mohi-al-Din, *Memories*, p 167
69 Lacoutures, *Egypt*, p 183
70 Mohi-al-Din, *Memories*, p 182
71 Mohi-al-Din, *Memories*, p 193-5
72 Stephens, *Nasser*, p 127
73 Fathallah Mahrus, interview with the author, Cairo, 15 December 2003
74 Gamal Abd-al-Nasser, 'Speech given at a celebration of the Association of Train Drivers and Conductors', 31 March 1954, in Nasser, *Speeches and briefings*, Volume 2, p236
75 Nasser, *Speeches and briefings*, Volume 2, p 249
76 Stephens, *Nasser*, p 127
77 Anthony Nutting, *Nasser* (Constable, London: 1972) p 72
78 Gamal Abd-al-Nasser, 'Speech in Alexandria to celebrate the signing of the Evacuation Treaty', 26 October 1954, translated from audio recording in Arabic on the Nasser Foundation web site, www.nasser.org
79 Mitchell, *The Society*, p 152
80 Gamal Abd-al-Nasser, 'Speech given in Port Said stadium', 23 December 1958, in Gamal Abd-al-Nasser, *Presidential speeches*, Dar al-Hilal, Cairo, no date (?1959), in Arabic, p 477
81 Stephens, *Nasser*, p 187
82 Nasser, *Philosophy*, p 85
83 Nasser, *Philosophy*, p 85
84 Nasser, *Philosophy*, p 88
85 Said Aburish, *Nasser: the last Arab* (Duckworth, London: 2004), p 201
86 Nasser, *Philosophy*, p 92
87 Nasser apparently later admitted that he had never actually read Pirandello's work.
88 Nasser, *Philosophy*, p 92
89 'All Nasser's children', Mona El-Ghobashy, *Cairo Times*, 6-12 January 2000
90 Mahmoud Murad, 'A stalwart of journalism', *Al-Ahram Weekly*, 2-8 October 2003
91 P. J. Vatikiotis, *The Egyptian army in politics – patterns for new nations?* (Indiana University Press, Bloomington: 1961) p 32
92 Lord Trevelyan, 'Nasser the visionary', *The Times*, 25 Jul 1970
93 'Runaway schoolboy enjoys his visit to Egypt', Pathé News reel, 25 April 1955, www.britishpathe.com
94 Peter Sluglett and Marion Farouk-Sluglett, *Iraq since 1958* (I B Tauris, London: 1987), p 309
95 Quoted in Lacouture, *Nasser*, p 90
96 Gamal Abd-al-Nasser, 'Speech given at the Bandung Conference 19 April 1955', transcribed from audio recording in English on the Nasser Foundation web site, www.nasser.org
97 Tabitha Petran, *Syria*, (Ernest Benn, London: 1972), p106
98 Quoted in David Hirst, *The Gun and the Olive Branch* (Faber and Faber, London: 1977) p 199
99 Stephens, *Nasser*, p 191
100 'Possible effects on Arab attitudes towards the unified plan and a Palestine settlement, and potential effects on the 'Cold War' posture of Syria,

Lebanon, Jordan and Iraq if large scale economic aid is given to Egypt at this juncture', State Department's Office of Near Eastern Affairs, 23 December 1953, published by George Washington University, available online at http://www.gwu.edu/~nsarchiv/NSAEBB/NSAEBB78/propagandapercent20117.pdf

101 *Al-Ahram Weekly*, Cairo, 10-16 May 2001

102 Trevelyan, 'Nasser the visionary', *The Times*, 25 July 1970

103 Gamal Abd-al-Nasser, 'Speech at the inauguration of the oil pipeline on the fourth anniversary of the revolution', 24 July 1956, translated from audio recording in Arabic on the Nasser Foundation web site, www.nasser.org

104 Lacoutures, *Egypt*, p 471

105 Lacoutures, *Egypt*, p 472, quotes from Nasser's speech retranslated from Gamal Abd-al-Nasser, Nationalisation speech, 26 July 1956, translated from audio recording in Arabic on the Nasser Foundation web site, www.nasser.org

106 Muhammad Hassanein Heikal, *Cutting the Lion's Tail: Suez through Egyptian eyes* (Andre Deutsch, London: 1986) p132

107 Lacoutures, *Egypt*, p 473

108 Lacoutures, *Egypt*, p 475

109 Gamal Abd-al-Nasser, 'Press conference', 12 August 1956, in English, transcribed from audio recording in English on the Nasser Foundation web site, www.nasser.org

110 The full text of the ultimatum can be found in 'Operation Musketeer: a military success ends in political failure', Major R. W. Rathburn, War since 1945 seminar, Marine Corps Command and Staff College, 1984, published at http://www.globalsecurity.org/military/library/report/1984/RRW.htm

111 Heikal, *Lion's Tail*, p 179

112 Stephens, *Nasser*, p 230

113 Gamal Abd-al-Nasser, 'Speech in Al-Azhar', 2 November 1956, Nasser, *Speeches and briefings*, p 1466

114 Clive Holes, *Modern Standard Arabic* (Longman, London: 1995) p 283-4

115 Lacoutures, *Egypt*, p 490

116 Mohi-al-Din, *Memories*, p 242

117 Lacouture, *Nasser*, p 353

118 John Badeau, 'Biographical note on Nasser and Naguib', in Gamal Abd-al-Nasser, *The Philosophy of the Revolution* (Economica Books, Buffalo:1959) p 82

119 Lacouture, *Nasser*, p 376

120 Shoukri, *Portrait*, p 38

121 Shoukri, *Portrait*, p 38

122 Holes, *Modern Standard Arabic*, p 286

123 Gamal Nkrumah, 'Safeguarding Nasser's legacy', *Al-Ahram Weekly*, 18-24 July 2002

124 Aburish, *Nasser*, p 235

125 Gamal Abd-al-Nasser, 'Speech announcing union of Egypt and Syria', 1 February 1958, translated from audio recording in Arabic on the Nasser Foundation web site, www.nasser.org

126 Patrick Seale, *The Struggle for Syria* (I B Tauris, London: 1986), p 321

127 Stephens, *Nasser*, p 277

128 Seale, *Syria*, London, p 321

129 Seale, *Syria*, London, p 322

130 Quoted in Petran, *Syria*, p128

131 Gamal Abd-al-Nasser, 'Speech given in Damascus', 1958, in Nasser, *Presidential speeches*, p 252

132   Hanna Batatu, *The old social classes and the revolutionary movements of Iraq* (Princeton University Press, Princeton:1978), p 816

133   Batatu, *The old social classes*, p 818

134   Batatu, *The old social classes*, p 816

135   Batatu, *The old social classes*, p 817

136   Aburish, *Nasser*, p 170

137   Gamal Abd-al-Nasser, 'Speech in Damascus', 13 March 1959, translated from audio recording in Arabic on the Nasser Foundation web site, www.nasser.org

138   Nasser, 'Speech in Damascus', 13 March 1959

139   Gamal Abd-al-Nasser, 'Speech to transport workers', 29 April 1954, translated from audio recording in Arabic on the Nasser Foundation web site, www.nasser.org

140   Nasser, 'Speech in Damascus', 13 March 1959

141   Robert Mabro and Samir Radwan, *The Industrialization of Egypt 1939-1975* (Clarendon Press, Oxford:1978) p 43

142   Mabro and Radwan, *Industrialization of Egypt*, p 87

143   Warriner, *Land Reform*, p 49-54

144   John Waterbury, *The Egypt of Nasser and Sadat: the political economy of two regimes* (Princeton University Press: 1983) p 70

145   Gamal Abd-al-Nasser, 'Speech 5 October 1961', translated from the Arabic transcript on the Nasser Foundation web site, www.nasser.org

146   Waterbury, *Political Economy*, p 75

147   Waterbury, *Political Economy*, p 75

148   Waterbury, *Political Economy*, p 78

149   Waterbury, *Political Economy*, p 78

150   *Bourse egyptienne*, 13 February 1960, quoted in Patrick O'Brien, The revolution in Egypt's economic system, (Oxford University Press: London, 1966), p125

151   Raymond Hinnebusch, *Egyptian politics under Sadat*, (Lynne Rienner: Boulder, 1988) p23-4

152   Petran, *Syria*, p 147

153   Quoted in Malcolm Kerr, *The Arab Cold War*, (Royal Institute of International Affairs, London: 1965) p 36

154   Steven Heydemann, *Authoritarianism in Syria: institutions and social conflict 1946 – 1970* (Cornell University Press, Ithaca: 1999) p 88

155   Heydemann, *Authoritarianism*, p 91

156   Stephens, *Nasser*, p 385

157   Kerr, *Cold War*, p 51

158   Kerr, *Cold War*, p 52

159   See for example Hinnebusch, *Egyptian Politics*, p 34

160   Quoted in Helena Cobban, *The Palestinian Liberation Organisation* (Cambridge University Press, Cambridge: 1983) p28-29

161   Quoted in Hirst, *The Gun*, p 215

162   Quoted in Hirst, *The Gun*, p 216

163   Richard B. Parker, *The Politics of Miscalculation in the Middle East* (Indiana University Press, Bloomington: 1993), p 5

164   Parker, *Politics of Miscalculation*, p 48

165   United Nations Security Council meeting, 5 June 1967, (S/Agenda/1347/Rev.1) http://domino.un.org/UNISPAL.NSF/9a798adbf322aff38525617b006d88d7/cd0beba6a1e28eff0525672800567b2c!OpenDocument

166   Gamal Abd-al-Nasser, 'Statement by President Gamal Abd-al-Nasser announcing his resignation as president', 9 June 1967, translated from the Arabic the Nasser Foundation web site, www.nasser.org

167 Gamal Abd-al-Nasser, 'Speech to mark Iraq's inclusion in the defence agreement between Egypt and Jordan', 4 June 1967, translated from audio recording in Arabic on the Nasser Foundation web site, www.nasser.org

168 Harry Hopkins, *Egypt the crucible: the unfinished revolution in the Arab world* (Houghton Mifflin, Boston: 1970), p 488

169 Heikal, quoted in Stephens, *Nasser*, p 497

170 Nasser, 'Resignation statement', 9 June 1967

171 Stephens, *Nasser*, p 506

172 Stephens, *Nasser*, p 507

173 Anouar Abdel-Malik, *Egypt: Military Society* (Vintage Books, New York: 1968) p ix

174 Stephens, *Nasser*, p 508

175 Gamal Abd-al-Nasser, 'Speech to mark celebrations of the fifteenth anniversary of the revolution', 23 July 1967, translated from the Arabic transcript on www.nasser.org

176 'FM Hakim Amer: Nasser's oldest comrade', *The Times*, 16 Sep 1967, p 12

177 Shoukri, *Portrait*, p 45

178 Abdel Magid Farid, *Nasser: the final years* (Ithaca Press, Reading: 1994) p 75

179 Shoukri, *Portrait*, p 45

180 Farid, *Nasser*, p 7

181 'Suicide by Egypt army leader', *The Times*, 16 Sept 1967

182 'Retrial ordered for Egyptian officers', *The Times*, Feb 27 1968

183 Lacouture, *Nasser*, p 321

184 Nutting, *Nasser*, p 457

186 Aburish, *Nasser*, p 277

186 Aburish, *Nasser*, p 277

187 Mustafa Abdel-Ghani, 'A shifting relationship', *Al-Ahram Weekly*, 18-24 July 2002

188 Muhammad Hassanein Heikal, *Road to Ramadan* (Collins, London: 1975) p 46-8

189 Heikal, *Ramadan*, p 87

190 Abdel Magid Farid, *Nasser*, p1

191 Heikal, *Ramadan*, p74

192 Gamal Nkrumah, 'Safeguarding Nasser's legacy', *Al-Ahram Weekly*, 18-24 July 2002

193 Heikal, *Ramadan*, p 63

194 Cobban, *PLO*, p 50

195 Heikal, *Ramadan*, p98

196 Quoted in Heikal, *Ramadan*, p 97

197 Stephens, *Nasser*, p 559

198 Hussein Abd-al-Razzaq, *Egypt on the 18/19 January* (Shadi, Cairo: no date – third edition), p 80, in Arabic

199 Nizar Qabbani, 'Gamal Abd-al-Nasser', *La*, 1971 translated from the Arabic, available on-line at http://www.damascus-online.com/poems/Nizar/Nasser.htm

200 Derek Hopwood, *Egypt: politics and society 1945-1990*, (London: Harper-Collins Academic, 1991) p112-3

201 Mohamed Hassanein Heikal, *Autumn of fury: the assassination of Sadat*, (New York: Random House, 1983) p183

202 Abd-al-Razzaq, *18/19 January*, p 80

203 Shoukri, *Portrait*, p 38

204 Tawfiq al-Hakim, *The Return of Conciousness* tr. Bayly Winder Macmillan, London 1985, p24

205 Al-Hakim, *The Return*, p 20

Chronology

Year	Age	Life
1918		born January 15 in Alexandria.
1935	18	Involved in school-student agitation for independence, injured during the protests and nearly expelled from school.
1937	19	Enters the military academy.
1944	26	Marries Tahia and settles down in Manshiet al-Bakry.
1948	30	Distinguishes himself as a young officer during Arab-Israeli War.
1952	34	Free Officers seize power July 23, announce land reform in September.
1954	36	Struggle for power with Muhammad Naguib, Nasser becomes prime minister.

Chronology

Year	History	Culture
1918	In Russia, Tsar Nicholas II and family executed. 11 November: Armistice agreement ends First World War. 'Spanish flu' epidemic kills at least 20m people in Europe, US and India.	Oswald Spengler, *The Decline of the West*, Volume 1. Amédée Ozenfant and Le Corbusier, *Après le Cubisme*. Paul Klee, *Gartenplan*.
1935	In Germany, Nuremberg Laws enacted. Philippines becomes self-governing. Italy invades Ethiopia.	George Gershwin, *Porgy and Bess*. Marx Brothers, *A Night at the Opera*
1937	Japan invades China: Nanjing massacre. Arab-Jewish conflict in Palestine..	Jean-Paul Sartre, *La Nausée*. John Steinbeck, *Of Mice and Men*. Picasso, *Guernica*
1944	Allies land in Normandy: Paris is liberated. Civil war in Greece.	*Lay My Burden Down* (documentary about former slaves). Adorno and Horkheimer's essay on the 'Culture Industry'
1948	Marshall plan (until 1951). Soviet blockade of Western sectors of Berlin: US and Britain organize airlift. In South Africa, Apartheid legislation passed. Gandhi is assassinated. State of Israel founded.	Brecht, *The Caucasian Chalk Circle*. Greene, *The Heart of the Matter*. Norman Mailer, *The Naked and the Dead*. Alan Paton, *Cry, the Beloved Country*. Vittorio De Sica, *Bicycle Thieves*
1952	European Coal and Steel Community formed; Britain refuses to join. US tests hydrogen bomb. Elisabeth II becomes queen of Britain. McCarthy era begins in US.	Michael Tippett, *The Midsummer Marriage*. Hemingway, *The Old Man and the Sea*. Samuel Beckett, *Waiting for Godot*. *High Noon* (starring Gary Cooper and Grace Kelly)
1954	Insurrection in Algeria. French withdrawal from Indochina: Ho Chi Minh forms government in North Vietnam.	Kingsley Amis, *Lucky Jim*. J R R Tolkien, *The Lord of the Rings*. Bill Haley and the Comets, 'Rock Around the Clock'

Year	Age	Life
1956	38	Confirmed as president in a referendum. Announces the nationalisation of the Suez Canal, faces attack by Britain, France and Israel.
1958	40	Leads Egypt into unity with Syria to form the United Arab republic; welcomes the outbreak of revolution in Iraq.
1961	43	The UAR collapses, Nasser launches a wave of nationalisations and takes over property of the private sector bourgeoisie.
1967	49	Six day war with Israel, Nasser resigns as president 9 June but withdraws his resignation a day later.
1970	52	Dies from a heart attack, September 28 following an Arab summit over the crisis in Jordan between King Hussein and Yasser Arafat.

Year	History	Culture
1956	Nikita Khruschev denounces Stalin. Suez Crisis. Revolts in Poland and Hungary. Fidel Castro and Ernesto 'Che' Guevara land in Cuba. Transatlantic telephone service links US to UK.	Lerner (lyrics) and Loewe (music), *My Fair Lady*. Elvis Presley, 'Heartbreak Hotel', 'Hound Dog', 'Love Me Tender'. John Osborne, *Look Back in Anger*
1958	Fifth French Republic; Charles De Gaulle becomes president. Great Leap Forward launched in China (until 1960). Castro leads communist revolution in Cuba.	Boris Pasternak, *Dr Zhivago*. Claude Lévi-Strauss, *Structural Anthropology*. Harold Pinter, *The Birthday Party*.
1961	Berlin Wall erected. Bay of Pigs invasion. Yuri Gagarin is first man in space.	The Rolling Stones are formed. Rudolf Nureyev defects from USSR.
1967	Six day War. First heart transplant.	The Beatles, *Sergeant Pepper's Lonely Hearts Club Band*. Gabriel García Márquez, *One Hundred Years of Solitude*. Tom Stoppard, *Rosencrantz and Guildenstern are Dead*.
1970	Severe fighting between Israel and Syria on Golan Heights. Iraq recognizes Kurdish autonomy, thus ending nine-year war. First-ever meeting of East and West German heads of government. Jordanian army disbands Palestinian militia. Syrian tanks invade Jordan in support of the Palestinians.	David Hockney, *Mr and Mrs Ossie Clark and Percy*. Michael Tippett, *The Knot Garden*. The Beatles, *Let It Be*. The Beatles officially split up, all four of them releasing solo albums. Simon and Garfunkel, *Bridge Over Troubled Water*. Death from drug overdose of superstar guitarist Jimi Hendrix.

Sources and transliteration

This account has drawn on the work of Nasser's other biographers, in particular studies by *Observer* journalist Robert Stephens and French writers Jean and Simone Lacouture. Other key sources include the memoirs of fellow Free Officers, Khaled Mohi-al-Din and Muhammad Naguib, and the writings of Nasser's confidant Muhammad Hassanein Heikal.

I have translated the bulk of Nasser's speeches quoted in this volume either from the extensive audio recordings available on the Nasser Foundation's web site www.nasser.org or other transcripts. Existing English translations of Nasser's speeches rarely do justice to their power, as he often departed from his prepared text, and because the published versions were frequently 'tidied up' to satisfy the conventions of written standard Arabic, even when Nasser himself often used Egyptian dialect when speaking. The key to Nasser's rhetoric lies in his mastery of the different registers of Arabic, from the baladi tongue of the Egyptian street to the language of international diplomacy.

A prolific speaker, Nasser rarely wrote at greater length than a newspaper article. His pamphlet, *The Philosophy of the Revolution*, is not only a crucial source for his political ideas, but also contains important biographical material. The *Philosophy* quickly became a bestseller in Egypt, and as Nasser's fame grew was translated into several other languages. Where these contemporary translations are of poor quality, I have re-translated the Arabic text, taken from the 9th edition of the paperback published by Dar al-Sha'ab in Cairo.

I have also drawn on my interviews with Ahmad Hamroush, one of the Free Officers who was close to the Communist group the

Democratic Movement for National Liberation (DMNL); Rifa'at al-Sa'id, now a leader of the left-wing Tagammu Party, but who joined the DMNL as a teenager in the late 1940s; and Fathallah Mahrus, a trade union activist who was imprisoned by the Free Officers during the 1950s.

Archival sources used here include the archives of the Communist Party of Great Britain held at the National Museum of Labour History in Manchester, and newspaper archives at the National Library in Cairo and Alexandria Municipal Library.

As far as possible I have followed published English usage in transliterating personal and place names, while rationalising the spelling of some common names. When referring to Egyptian places or people I have also rendered the Arabic letter 'jim', as a 'g', following Egyptian pronunciation. Thus Jamal 'Abd-an-Nasir is rendered Gamal Abd-al-Nasser and Muhammad Najib is rendered Muhammad Naguib.

Anne Alexander,
London 2004

Selected further reading in English

Works by Nasser

The Philosophy of the Revolution is out of print in English, although easily available from second-hand booksellers. It has often been poorly translated, however.

Other biographies

Said Aburish, *Nasser: the last Arab* (Duckworth, London: 2004)
Jean Lacouture, *The Demigods: charismatic leadership in the Third World*, (Alfred A. Knopf, New York: 1970)
Jean Lacouture, *Nasser* (Secker and Warburg, London: 1973)
Anthony Nutting, *Nasser* (Constable, London: 1972)
Robert Stephens, *Nasser* (Penguin, London: 1971)

Memoirs

Hassanein Heikal, *Cutting the Lion's Tail: Suez through Egyptian eyes* (Andre Deutsch, London: 1986)
Muhammad Hassanein Heikal, *Road to Ramadan* (Collins, London: 1975)
Khaled Mohi-al-Din, *Memories of a Revolution* (American University in Cairo Press, Cairo: 1995)
Muhammad Naguib, *Egypt's Destiny* (Victor Gollancz, London:1955),
Anwar Sadat, *In search of identity – an autobiography* (Harper and Row, New York: 1977)Muhammad

History

Anouar Abdel-Malik, *Egypt. Military Society* (Vintage Books, New York: 1968)

Abdel Magid Farid, *Nasser: the final years* (Ithaca Press, Reading: 1994)
David Hirst, *The Gun and the Olive Branch* (Faber and Faber, London: 1977)

Derek Hopwood, *Egypt: politics and society 1945-1990*, (London: Harper-Collins Academic, 1991)

Malcolm Kerr, *The Arab Cold War*, (Royal Institute of International Affairs, London: 1965)

Joel Beinin and Lockman, *Workers on the Nile* (Princeton University Press, Princeton, NJ: 1988)

Jean and Simone Lacouture, *Egypt in Transition* (Methuen, London: 1958)

Richard P. Mitchell, *The Society of the Muslim Brothers* (Oxford University Press, London: 1969)

Gilles Perrault, *A Man Apart: a Life of Henri Curiel* (Zed Books, London: 1987)

Tabitha Petran, *Syria*, (Ernest Benn, London: 1972)

Ghali Shoukri, *Egypt: portrait of a president – Sadat's road to Jerusalem* (Zed Books, London: 1981)

P. J. Vatikiotis, *A History of Modern Egypt* (Weidenfeld and Nicolson, London: 1991),

Political economy

Raymond Hinnebusch, *Egyptian politics under Sadat*, (Lynne Rienner: Boulder, 1988)

Robert Mabro and Samir Radwan, *The Industrialization of Egypt 1939-1975* (Clarendon Press, Oxford: 1978)

John Waterbury, *The Egypt of Nasser and Sadat*: the political economy of two regimes (Princeton University Press: 1983)

Literature

Paul Starkey, *From the Ivory Tower: A critical study of Tawfiq al-Hakim* (Ithaca press, Reading: 1987)

Tawfiq al-Hakim, *The Maze of Justice* (Saqi Books, London: 1989)

Tawfiq al-Hakim, *Return of the Spirit* (Lynne Rienner, Boulder: 1990)

Tawfiq al-Hakim, *The Return of Conciousness* tr. Bayly Winder (Macmillan, London:1985)

The novelist Naguib Mahfouz wrote two novels which deal with the contradictions of Egyptian society under Nasser which are available in English.

Naguib Mahfouz, *The Thief and the Dogs*, (The American University in Cairo Press, Cairo: 1999)

Naguib Mahfouz, *Miramar*, (The American University in Cairo Press, Cairo: 1998)

Picture sources

The author and publishers wish to express their thanks to the following sources of illustrative material and/or permission to reproduce it. They will make proper acknowledgements in future editions in the event that any omissions have occurred.

Egypt Historical Archive: pp. i, iii, iv, 2, 6-7, 9, 15, 21, 23, 24, 28, 34, 39, 45, 48, 51, 53, 60, 69, 73, 81, 85, 89, 91, 92, 95, 101, 102, 103, 105, 120, 136, 138, 141, 148, 153, 156, 158, 163, 164; Michael Haag: pp. 11

Index

Faust, Jean-Jacques, 94
fedayeen, 37, 38
fellahin, 4, 6–7, 8, 17, 53, 126
Fiqi, Hassan al-, 134
FLN, 70, 81–2
France, 4, 8, 12, 19; commercial interests
    in Egypt, 118–19; decolonization, 70;
    Algerian war, 81–2; Suez Crisis, 82,
    87–90, 93, 95–6, 119, 139
Free Officers, 8, 23–4, 27, 29–30, 140, 157;
    emergence, 35–7; contest Officers'
    Club elections, 37–8; emergence of
    Nasser, 40–1; revolution of 1952 and
    subsequent regime, 41–64, 71–2, 75–9,
    81, 106, 137; 'blessed movement',
    56–7, 159; changes in Nasser's relations
    with, 97–8, 113–14, 123, 143, 145;
    ideas on economics, 117; lifestyles,
    130, 142; accelerated promotions, 147
Fu'ad, Ahmad, 29, 47, 54
Fu'ad, King, 13–14

Gadaffy, Mu'ammar al-, 153
Garibaldi, Giuseppe, 16
Gaza, 131, 133
Gaza Strip, 33, 47; Israeli raid, 79–80; falls
    to Israelis, 135
Geneva, 66, 97
Ghana, 127
Gladstone, William Ewart, 5
Golan Heights, 133, 139, 158
Gulf of Aqaba, 134

Habash, George, 151
Hadi, Isma'il Abd-al-, 35
Hakim, Tawfiq al-, 16–18, 36; biography,
    16; reappraisal of Nasser, 159
Hamroush, Ahmad, 32, 53
Hasan, Abd-al-Fattah, 38
Hashemite dynasty, 76, 77, 109, 112
Hebron, 135
Heikal, Muhammad Hassanein, 74–6, 88,
    90, 145, 147, 149; biography, 75; on
    ceasefire negotiations with Palestinians,
    152–3; on Sadat, 156
Hejaz, the, 3
Helwan, 14
Heydemann, Robert, 125
Hilali, Naguib, 40
Hinnebusch, Raymond, 123
Hitler, Adolf, 85, 86
Hodeiby, Hasan al-, 57, 67
Hungary, 96
Husni, Ahmad Saleh, 22
Hussein, Abd al-Nasser, 8–9, 15; remar-
    ries, 14
Hussein, Ahmad, 14, 19

Hussein, Fahima, 9; death, 14
Hussein, Kamal-al-Din, 35
Hussein, Khalil, 9, 10, 14
Hussein, King, of Jordan, 133, 137, 151–4
Hussein, Saddam, 146
Hussein, Sharif, 77
Hussein, Taha, 15

Ibrahim, Hasan, 35
India, 78, 127
infitah, 157
International Monetary Fund, 123–4, 160
Iran, 88, 113
Iraq, 70–1, 76–7, 80, 88, 152; Ba'ath
    Party, 72, 114, 129; Communists,
    109, 114–15, 117, 129; invasion of,
    160, 162; joins defence pact, 137; rev-
    olution, 109–12, 113; and UAR,
    113–15; under Saddam Hussein, 146
Iraq Petroleum Company (IPC), 80, 95
Iskra, 31
Islam, 15, 18, 24, 30, 50, 57, 72, 74
Islamic Jihad, 156, 159
Islamist movement, 162
Ismail, Khedive, 4, 156
Ismailiyya, 37, 38, 84
Israel, 79, 82, 107, 152, 162; losses at
    Karameh, 150; negotiations with
    PLO, 160; peace with Egypt, 156,
    159, 160; prohibited from Suez Canal,
    87; right to exist and Rogers Plan,
    150–1; role in Suez Crisis, 88–90, 93,
    96, 105, 139; run-up to Six Day War,
    131–4; Six Day War, 135–7, 139,
    147, 151; war of 1973, 158
Israel Radio, 134
Israelis, 33–5, 79, 133, 110, 147, 152

Jabal Amil, 110
jahiliyya, 162
Jerusalem, 109, 136, 138, 159
Jones, Howard, 75–6
Jordan, 76, 80, 111; civil war, 152–3; joins
    defence pact, 137
Jordan, River, 132
Judaism, 72
July Decrees, 121–2
Jumblatt, Kamal, 111

Kafr al-Dawwar, 51
Kafr al-Zayyat oil company, 19
Karameh, 150
Kazim, Tahia Muhammad, *see* Nasser, Tahia
    Muhammad
Kennedy, John F, 124
Kenya, 70
Kerr, Malcolm, 129

liamentary government, 61; becomes Prime Minister, 65, 67; assassination attempt, 68, 83; role as leader of Arab world, 69, 71–2, 96–7, 108, 150; religion, 74, 97; becomes President, 83; emerges as Al-Ra'is, 97–100, 145; 'metaphysical union' with Egyptian people, 98, 144; formation and collapse of UAR, 104, 107–9, 114–15, 124–5; opposition to Communism, 116; suspicion and single-mindedness, 122; and Six Day War, 134, 136–7, 139–40; resignation, 140; withdraws resignation, 141–2; moves against the 'new class', 143–4; protests against, 144–5; personal dictatorship, 146; ill health, 149, 154; ambivalent attitude to Palestinian guerrillas, 150; death, 154; funeral, 155–6